Growing Up with the Philadelphia Zoo

The 125th anniversary of the Philadelphia Zoo is a time of great pride for Mellon Bank. We have enjoyed watching and helping the Zoo as it has grown over the years. After all, as a Pennsylvania bank founded in 1869, we're from the same generation of Pennsylvania institutions that saw the Zoo open its gates in 1874.

The Philadelphia Zoo is a place that fosters diversity, where families from all walks of life come together to appreciate nature. Experiences at the Zoo bring dreams to life, inspire imaginations, and help young minds grow strong.

At Mellon, sponsoring this limited-edition publication of America's First Zoostory, *and knowing that the proceeds will help support the Zoo's mission of conservation, education, recreation, and science, makes us proud.*

Mellon is pleased to join you in supporting the Philadelphia Zoo. Our employees are your neighbors–people who know you and the community, people who are dedicated to serving your financial needs and making the region a better place. We congratulate Clark DeLeon on a wonderful book and the Philadelphia Zoo on 125 years of bringing the wonders of nature to generations in the Delaware Valley.

William J. Stallkamp
Vice Chairman
Mellon Bank Corporation

Mellon

Girard Avenue Entrance with Frank Furness's gatehouses, circa 1876.

America's First ZOOSTORY

125 YEARS AT THE PHILADELPHIA ZOO

by Clark DeLeon

THE
DONNING COMPANY
PUBLISHERS

To
Anne E. DeLeon
1911–1999
Because you were the best, Mom,
you were the best.

Dust jacket photo: Girard Avenue Gates, circa 1935.
Hand-painted glass slide from Zoo Archives.

For information, write:
The Donning Company/Publishers
184 Business Park Drive, Suite 106
Virginia Beach, VA 23462

Steve Mull, General Manager
Jackie Trudel-Lane, Project Director
Dawn V. Kofroth, Assistant General Manager
Richard A. Horwege, Senior Editor
Kevin M. Brown, Art Director, Designer
Kelly M. Perkoski, Graphic Designer
John Harrell, Imaging Artist
Teri S. Arnold, Director of Marketing

Library of Congress Cataloging-in-Publication Data
DeLeon, Clark, 1949–
America's first zoostory: 125 years at the Philadelphia Zoo / Clark DeLeon
p.   cm.
ISBN 1-57864-069-5 (hardcover : alk. paper)
1. Philadelphia Zoological Garden—History.   I. Title.
QL76.5.U62P484   1999
590'.7'374811—dc21   99-24040
CIP

Printed in the United States of America

CONTENTS

I wish this book was longer. I really do. In a longer book you would have heard more—more from and more about the people telling *America's First Zoostory* today.

Because of the unforgiving nature of time and space, I have left out too many names to mention, not to mention the names of people I never met. The guys in the parking lots, the ticket takers, the docents, the vice presidents in charge of important stuff, the long-time members, the generous corporate donors, and the freckled-faced lady with the red hair and the push broom who always had a big smile for me whenever I walked past.

I've left out big shots and the little shots: The day-trippers and the daily fixtures, the people who come and go and the people who came to stay, the people who are different and the people who are the difference.

What I have tried to do through the individuals whose names are mentioned, is to tell the story of the genuinely fond, unrelenting, unpredictable, laborious, sometimes fearful, frequently hilarious, and always respectful relationship between the animals in the garden and the humans who are the garden keepers. I have also tried to present the historical context of the times and of the city during the century plus two score years that America's first zoo has struggled and triumphed and struggled, again and again, to survive, to prosper and endure.

Interesting (I think) has been a common reaction among friends and acquaintances upon learning that I was writing a book about the zoo. "The Philadelphia Zoo," I'd offer. In response, the two most frequently asked questions to me were, "Are you going to write about the fire?" and "Are you going to talk about [morality of zoos]?" I say "morality of zoos" in brackets because that usually was the thrust of the question, if not the exact words.

Yes, I'd reply, I'll write about the fire. How could I not write about the fire that killed John and Jingga and Octavian and twenty other primates on Christmas Eve 1995. How could I not write about the single deadliest event in zoo history—not just this zoo, in any zoo's history!—how could I not describe the night Philadelphia's heart broke? And how the Zoo's heart has yet to mend?

Yes, I will write about the fire.

As for discussing the morality of zoos—Is it right to keep wild animals captive in an unnatural environment?—I believe it is a fair question with several unsatisfactory answers. Certainly the primary mission of zoos has undergone a dramatic core-shaking transformation in the last fifteen years. It is no longer about displaying animals for public amusement, although that is still an important part of the zoo's function. Today's zoos are on a conservation mission, a mission as specific as saving individual endangered species one genotype at a time. It may be too little too late for the thousands of

species driven into extinction each year under the heel of human progress. It may be nothing more than a finger in the dike attempting to hold back the inevitable flood. But it is a stand that has changed the way zoos view themselves and their responsibilities to the animals who live in the zoo and the humans who visit them.

Today, the vast majority of animals in the Philadelphia Zoo were bred in captivity. These are wild animals that have never lived in the wild. In zoos across the country, 93 percent of the mammals and 75 percent of the birds were zoo bred. Those animals still caught in the wild serve an important and irreplaceable role in enriching the genetic diversity of their species, which have vanished along with their habitat, whether it be rain forest, savannah, or tundra.

But, should humans in Philadelphia participate in genetic matchmaking of individuals representing an endangered species in Africa or Asia, a species all but extinct except within the bars, moats, and glass enclosures of zoos in Europe and North America? In other words, "Who died and named you Noah?"

In the spring of 1997 the Philadelphia Zoo launched an initiative—initiatives are always *launched* by the way, I can't say I know exactly why. I'd be perfectly happy with an initiative that simply started on cold mornings—called Vision 2020. Eighty people from different backgrounds with a personal stake in the future of the Zoo: staff, volunteers, board members, politicians, academics, community activists, conservationists, and friends of the Zoo met at the Academy of Music for a three-day conference in which they were invited to reinvent the idea of the Zoo.

Zoo President Pete Hoskins charged those attending the conference to create a shared vision of the Philadelphia Zoo for the next century. The results of that seminal conference are manifest in the Vision 2020 Master Plan, a breathtakingly ambitious building program unlike any the Zoo has undertaken before. The Philadelphia Zoo of the future will continue to celebrate the historic legacy and Victorian garden setting of America's first zoo, while completely retooling the infrastructure of exhibits and their educational objectives, with a recommitted focus on the comfort and enjoyment of guests (or "amusement-seeking strangers" as they were referred to by the Zoological Society's recording secretary in 1873).

The Zoo's "core purpose" in the future, as articulated by Vision 2020's committee-written draft, is to "Advance discovery, understanding and stewardship of the natural world through compelling exhibition and interpretation of living animals and plants." Its "vision," according to the draft, is "America's first zoo will be first in modeling and promoting a responsible and caring attitude toward all living things, inspiring learning and action beyond its gates." In a nutshell: Part Darwin, part Disney, part Francis of Assisi.

In the ever-escalating arguments over ethics, morality, and responsibility, zoos will suffer from the inevitable conclusion: The more zoos change, the more they remain the same. So be it.

When I consider the notion of a zero zoo world, and what would be lost to both individual animals and individual humans by the absence of zoos, I think of the *Starfish Story*. It goes like this:

Once there was an old man who stood on the ocean's edge staring into the enormous vastness stretching before him and pondering on his own fragile inconsequential existence. Before him lay tens of thousands of starfish washed up on shore and left to die by the retreating tide.

From the corner of his eye, the old man saw a young boy running from starfish to starfish and tossing each back into the life-giving sea. The old man watched the boy throw back a hundred starfish even as the waves deposited a thousand more onto the sand.

Finally, the old man could hold his tongue no longer. "Boy," he shouted, "can't you see that there are more starfish than you can ever save? You could work all day and all night and it wouldn't matter." The boy paused, bent over, and picked up another starfish. "It matters to this one," he said, turning and throwing it beyond the breakers.

In the face of global deforestation, species extinction, Third World industrialization, and the inevitable triumph of human greed over conscience, all the conservation efforts of all world's zoos put together are but one tireless little boy hurling hope into the shifting tides of history.

Does it matter?

It does to those you will meet in the following pages.

Sonny Woerner, Bird House keeper, after thirty-two years at the Zoo.

Chuck Ripka.

Ann Hess with bear cubs.

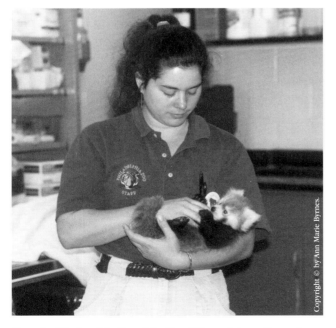

Copyright © by Ann Marie Byrnes.

Sandy Skeba-McCampbell with red panda cub.

In a way, this book is to the Zoo what the Zoo is to the animal world. It tells the story but there's not enough room to tell more than part of the story. And I would like to thank the many people who helped me tell the parts of *America's First Zoostory* that appear in these pages. First to Tom Hartman and Ann Marie Byrnes, whose wonderful photographs of animals in the Philadelphia Zoo speak volumes both about the Zoo's mission and the care the animals receive. I can't imagine what this book would be like without their gorgeous portraits of Zoo residents. Next I'd like to thank Kristen Lewis of the Zoo's Public Relations Department for her almost daily assistance during the research and writing of this book. Thanks also to PR Director Antoinette Maciolek and Senior Vice President for Marketing and Communication Fran Feldman for thinking of me when looking for an author and to Mellon Bank for funding this project. Major thanks to the many people at the Donning Company/Publishers—Senior Editor Richard Horwege, Art Director Kevin Brown, Designer Kelly Perkoski, General Manager Steve Mull, and Jackie Trudel-Lane—chief noodge and bottlewasher—for their hard work and commitment in bringing this book in on time under imposing deadline restrictions.

The list of truly zooper people who deserve thanks for their time, assistance, and generosity includes Tom Riggins, Pete Hoskins, Umar Mycka, Barry Lyngard, Adam Cheek, Karl Kranz, Jen Savage, John Ffinch, Sonny Woerner, Kim Whitman, Steve Cepregi, Suzie Gurley, Dr. Aliza Baltz, Dr. Donna Ialeggio-Pelletier, Ken Pelletier, Dr. Kevin Wright, Lynn Fulton, Bob Berghaier, Brian McCampbell, Chuck Ripka, Tim Hendrickson, Dr. Andy Baker, Beth Bahner, Marina Haynes, Dr. Keith Hinshaw, Tanya Minott, Charlie Sturts, Eileen Boyle, Rod Haines, Bob Pittman, Anita Primo, Reg Hoyt, Frances Andrews, Dell Fioravanti, Joyce Parker, Ken Rebechi, Susan Isackson, Sandy Skeba-McCampbell, Ron Fricke, Lisa Leete, Hank Caratura, Marilyn Hill, Barbara Toddes, Dr. John Trupkiewicz, Nancy McDonald, Mary Ward, and Ann Hess. I regret that because of space limitations more of their words and contributions were not included in this book.

Among the valuable sources of information about the Zoo cited in this book is the book *The Peaceable Kingdom* by John Sedgwick and *A Field Guide to the Life and Times of Roger Conant* by Roger Conant. Dr. Conant should also be thanked for his many articles appearing in Zoo publications during a period of more than three decades, as should the writings of former curator of mammals Fred Ulmer and former curator of birds John "Gus" Griswald. Thanks also to Jim Dougherty of Berry and Homer Inc. for photographic services. And a special thanks to Philadelphia artist Bill Bell for allowing me to share his ageless illustration of the Zoo of his boyhood.

Finally, thanks to my wife, Sara, and our children for putting up with me during this process. I was probably home more than I ever was, but I was never really there, if you know what I mean.

ACKNOWLEDGMENTS

Keeper and baboon.

Once upon a time long, long ago, before there was a City Hall, before there was a bronze hatted William Penn atop its tower; before there was an Art Museum or a Parkway or a Philadelphia Orchestra; before there was a Mummers Parade up Broad Street or a subway underneath it, before there was a Bryn Mawr or an Ardmore or a Narberth, before there was an Elkins Park or a Main Line or a Cherry Hill, before all of that and much more came into being, there was a zoological garden in Philadelphia. It was America's first zoo. This is its story. Like so many American firsts, it is a Philadelphia story. And like so many Philadelphia stories, it starts with long delays. But more on that later.

The Philadelphia Zoological Garden is a U.S. Centennial-era zoo on the threshold of the new millennium. We can assess its future by learning from its past. Throughout its history, Philadelphia as been the little engine that could of major American zoos. Over the years it has done more with less—money, land, government support, parking, you name it—than zoos twice its size. It has established an international reputation in the fields of nutrition, research into the cause of prevention of disease, first-time breeding, and longevity of certain species. And it accomplished these achievements virtually through the force of personality and commitment by members of the Zoo staff and Board of Directors over the years. Because of the opening of the anxiously awaited new Primate Reserve, this year is expected to be the most successful in Philadelphia Zoo history, a history that seemed to have peaked early—in 1876 it set an annual attendance record of 677,630 visitors that wasn't broken until 1951. In the last two decades the Zoo's annual attendance has topped a million, and this year's attendance is projected to hit 1.45 million. But this is also the year of the quasqui, as well as the gorilla, orang-utan, gibbon, and lemur. The grand opening hoopla over Primate Reserve has allowed the quasqui to arrive at the Zoo almost unnoticed. Over the years the Zoo has hosted its share of visiting exotics, from koalas to white alligators, but this will be the first quasqui in the Zoo's long collection of firsts. It is the first American zoo to celebrate its quasquicentennial—its 125th anniversary—from the day the Zoo opened to the public on July 1, 1874.

ZOO'S ON FIRST?

At a meeting of the zoological society last evening, plans for the proposed zoological garden in Fairmount Park were exhibited. For the purposes of this garden the park commissioners have set apart 32 acres in the West Park, just above the Girard Avenue Bridge. The location is a very suitable one, and if the garden is established and stocked with rare and curious animals, it will add very greatly to the attractions of our beautiful public pleasure grounds. The zoological garden in Central Park, New York, is one of the most interesting fea-

tures of that delightful place of public resort, and a similar one here will be equally well appreciated.

—From a report in the *Philadelphia Evening Telegraph*, Friday, January 17, 1873

No one disputes Philadelphia's rightful claim to the title America's first zoo, however, like the story of Adam and Eve in the Bible, the newspaper report quoted above does seem to beg certain questions. If Adam and Eve were the first people, who was that woman that Cain married after he killed Abel and fled to the land of Nod on the east of Eden? If Philadelphia was the first zoo, why would a local newspaper be touting the virtues of a zoological garden in Central Park a year before Philadelphia's opened? It all hinges on the accepted definition of the word *zoo.* As the late great Philadelphia Zoo President Bill Donaldson put it when asked about the menagerie in Central Park that opened in 1861, "One swan in a pond and one bear on a chain do not a zoo make." Philadelphia was the first zoo worthy of the name. The issue of which is Ameica's first zoo is settled beyond any argument by the March 21, 1859 incorporation date of the Zoological Society of Philadelphia—years before any other American city.

Animals had been placed on display in garden settings for thousands of years. In the fifteenth century B.C. Queen Hatshepsut of Egypt kept a collection that included monkeys, leopards, and a giraffe. Three thousand years ago the Chinese emperor created the "Park of Intelligence" containing a vast collection of animals and fish. Amsterdam exhibited lions in the 1400s and the first rhino seen in Europe in 1640. In the New World, exotic animals arrived with sailors returning from overseas voyages. Philadelphia saw its first lion in 1727, when a sailor put it on display at Abraham Bickley's store, charging an admission fee of one shilling per peek. A camel passed through town in 1740, and not long after that a moose and a leopard. When Philadelphia was the capital of the United States, a visiting entrepreneur put an elephant on display at Ninth and Market Streets, charging the curious four bits to see the lone pachyderm. In 1797, John Bill

It wasn't love at first sight for English writer Thomas Macauly.

Rickett's circus at Twelfth and Market Streets featured acts like the "Dancing Monkey," "The Card-Playing Dog," and the "Learned Pig."

But it wasn't until Charles Willson Peale opened his famous Natural History Museum, the "repository of natural curiosities" on the second floor of Independence Hall, that any sort of scientific approach was brought to the display of animals. In 1804, President Thomas Jefferson sent Peale two prairie dogs, the first ever seen in the East, that had been shipped back to Washington by Lewis and Clark during their exploration in search of the Northwest Passage. The president wanted Peale to inspire the imagination of the country by displaying animals from the American West. In 1808, Jefferson donated two young grizzly bears to Peale's collection. At first they were tethered by chain outdoors in Independence Square, but when they grew more powerful, Peale placed them in an iron cage adjoining Philosophical Hall across Fifth Street. One of the bears escaped, and had to be shot after it took refuge in the basement of the building. The other bit off the arm of a monkey that had playfully reached inside the cage. Peale's Museum was a combination of live animals, stuffed animals, and paintings. Its popularity faded in the early 1800s as the more scientific mission of its presentation was absorbed by the Academy of Natural Sciences, and its appeal to the ticket-buying public was usurped by flashier animal attractions offered up by circus operators.

The idea of a zoo didn't exist, let alone the word *zoo*. The first zoo worthy of that name was founded by the London Zoological Society in 1826 in Regents Park, a members-only garden that took itself quite seriously. Founders Sir Stamford Raffles and Sir Humphrey Davy declared that the animals on display in its zoological garden "would be objects of scientific research, not vulgar admiration." No Card-Playing Dogs here. But in 1847, the Zoological Society relented and began offering admission to nonmembers on weekdays for one shilling apiece. In 1850, 300,000 people turned out to see the first hippopotamus on display in London. To which writer Thomas Macauly remarked, "I have seen the Hippo both asleep and awake, and I can assure you that, asleep or awake, he is the ugliest of the works of God." (Obviously spoken by a man who had never seen a rhinoceros.) The word *zoo* as an abbreviation for zoological gardens didn't become common until after 1877, when it first appeared in the lyrics of a popular British song of that year—"Walking in the zoo is an OK thing to do." Two years later in an article on April 16, 1879 *Harper's New Monthly Magazine*, the word *zoo* was used in reference to the Philadelphia Zoological Gardens. "To Philadelphia belongs the honor of being the first American city to establish a fine zoological garden," *Harper's* wrote. "It was opened on July 1, 1874. Indeed, there is no other in the country yet that has any pretensions of being a real zoological garden."

THE BIG D

On the day I arrived at the garden to begin working on this book, the first thing I noticed about the Zoo—after all these years—is that it is shaped like a Big D. Understand this and you'll never get lost in the Zoo. The straight part of the D runs north and south on Thirty-fourth Street from Girard Avenue to the railroad bridge. The curved part of the D is created by the merging of a dozen train tracks carrying city-bound freight from the west and passengers from the north, including the regular Amtrak trains heading to New York and Boston from Thirtieth Street Station. Fittingly, perhaps, the larger boundary of Philadelphia's nineteenth-century zoo, is literally defined by the dominant technology of the nineteenth century—the steam-powered locomotive. The curve begins at the south end, the top part of the Big D, where a bridge takes Thirty-fourth Street auto traffic over the railroad tracks. At the top of the curve the freight track continues west parallel to the river and the passenger lines continue to curve north until meeting the lower part of the D at Girard Avenue where an ancient stone arched bridge takes the trains over Girard Avenue, the Schuylkill Expressway, West River Drive, and the Schuylkill River. Running just inside the curve between the railroad tracks and the zoo proper is a surface road called Zoological Drive, along which most of the Zoo's service, maintenance, employee, and delivery entrances are located.

If you enter from the North Gate, turning left takes you down the straight line of the Big D past the llamas, cavies, anteaters, polar bears, red pandas, otters, penguins, zebras, gazelles, giraffes, and warthogs. Bearing right from the same entrance takes you along the curve of the D and you'll pass lemurs, langurs, bats, colobus monkeys, naked mole rats, kangaroos, hippos, Galapagos tortoises, king cobras, gila monsters, poison tree frogs, crocodiles, hippos, rhinos, elephants, gorillas, orangutans, gibbons, lions, tigers, leopards, camels, lorikeets, the Children's Zoo, golden pheasants, wild dogs, and cheetahs before eventually linking up with straight line at the top of the Big D at the South Gate entrance Gate House.

Think Big D and the Zoo makes sense, sort of. At least along the perimeter or the Main Path as it's called. Enter the vast middle of the zoo with its meandering pathways and all bets are off. The Bermuda Triangle is easier to explain—or escape. I have watched visitors poring over their maps like GIs during the Battle of the Bulge trying to figure out which sign's arrow *really* points towards to the lions. From the interior of the Big D, Zoo signs are as helpful as the Scarecrow's directions to Dorothy along the Yellow Brick Road. The Emerald City is thataway.

Then again, it could be *thataway*. Credit (or blame) for the series of circles, curlicues, round-abouts, and diagonal pathways through the middle of the zoo should probably go to the original designer, Herman J. Schwarzmann, chief engineer of the Zoological Society, whose mid-1870s layout of buildings and pedestrian walkways served as the template for all future designs.

For the most part the Big D design has served the Zoo well. For a century and a quarter, visitors entering the North Gate have known that the lions and tigers and elephants and reptiles are straight ahead along the curve of the Big D (in different buildings, of course, and slightly different locations). The bears have always been exactly where the are today along the path that leads to the left from the North Entrance. So has *Solitude*, John Penn's summer estate, which hasn't moved an inch in more than two hundred years. But over the years much has changed along the area of the Zoo closest to Thirty-fourth Street where the parking lot, Administration Building, Carnivore Kingdom, and African Plains are today. Gone are the ten paddocks holding yaks and deer and musk ox and cape buffalo and elk and wild sheep and wildebeest and aoudads and reindeer. Gone from the Zoo entirely are animals and exhibits that were fixtures for decades from Monkey Island to the Sea Lion Ponds, from the Beaver Pond to the Monkey House. Despite this, life within the Big D seems reassuringly familiar. The garden itself is an ever-changing and never-changing presence. From the moment you walk past that achingly sad and almost unbearably sweet statue of the *Dying Lioness* pierced by a hunter's arrow and enter the North Entrance between those signature gate houses designed by Frank Furness, you feel like you have returned to the zoo of your childhood. Even if you've never been here before.

It's deja zoo, all over again.

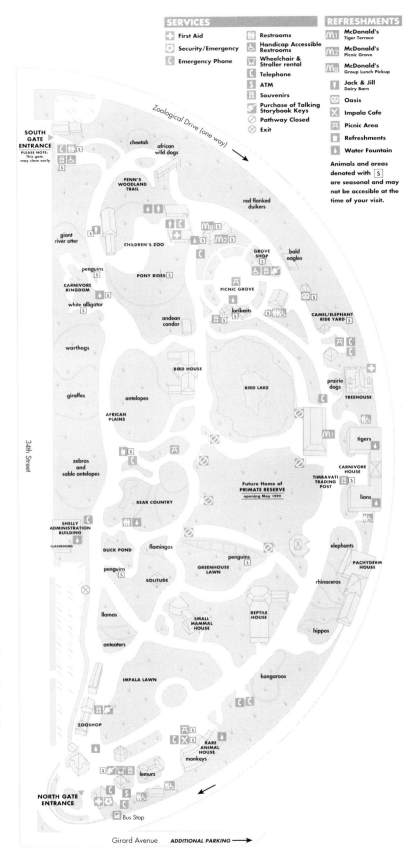

What a Face! *This douc langur from the mountains of Vietnam lives in the Rare Animal House.*

Greeters at the
Members Entrance.

ZooShop volunteers.

Keepers Joyce Parker and Michelle Jamison from the Reptile House.

Andy Baker, curator of primates and small mammals, with volunteers.

"The past is not dead," William Faulkner *wrote. "It isn't even past." A walk around the Philadelphia Zoo is a reminder that the past is still present. There is a feel about the place that is timeless, familiar, comforting. Yes, you* have *been here before. As a child. As a young adult. As a parent. As a grandparent. There is something about the contours of the Zoo, something in the way the main pathway seems to bend toward infinity, the way the animals reveal themselves along its arc. Illustrator and commercial artist Bill Bell grew up in West Philadelphia during the late 1930s and early 1940s. The charming Zoo in his memory is captured in this wonderful illustration that appeared in his book* The Saxophone Boy.

Junior Zoo Apprentice Program participant Gordon Branham helps an African schoolboy during a JZAP visit to Kenya in 1998.

Dan McNellis, elephant keeper.

Copyright © by Tom Dewey.

Keeper Doug Radjiewicz entices a wallaby to play.

*Bob Wolcott, former
Board chairman,
holds Kanya the
white lion cub.*

The Pride of Philadelphia:
The Zoo's four adult lions (above) relax in the outdoor grotto of the Carnivora House. From left are Zenda, Merlin, Vinkel, and Jezebel.

Pride of the Pride:
Hundreds of thousands flocked to the Zoo to see the white lion cubs (right) Kanya, Kolwa, and Tandi after they were born in 1995.

Copyright © by Tom Hartman.

Copyright © by Tom Hartman.

Leaping Lantar: *Lantar the Siberian tiger loves to dive into the moat of the Tiger Grotto.*

Snow Stalker: *Lantar's son, Al the Siberian tiger, seems to prefer colder weather.*

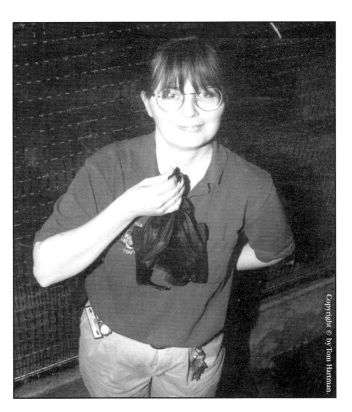

Keeper Jo Anne Kowalski and Angus, a Rodriguez fruit bat.

Zoo guides help visitors, 1994.

Scott Bartow with colobus monkeys.

Zoo volunteers Tom Gaughn and Jeanne Segal, retired vice president, in the Zoo's Greenhouse.

Spirit of America: *Ritz the bald eagle spreads his wings in the Eagle Flight Exhibit.*

Nice Hat! *Victoria crested pigeons, the world's largest pigeons, have an exquisite shock of feathers on top of their heads.*

Colors Anyone? Flamingos care for their young in the nesting area of the Flamingo Yard.

Keeper Teri Maas-Anger.

*Florence Robin, member of
the Camera Club, in 1993.*

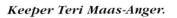

*Zoo docent Jeanette Decker
talks to students in 1986.*

A typical busy day at the Treehouse.

**Maria Schwalbe and mongoose
lemur.**

Banana Treat: *Twenty-six-year-old Curator of Reptiles Roger Conant feeds a Galapagos tortoise, circa 1936, in the Reptile House. Photo, a hand-painted glass slide, from Zoo Archives.*

A Man and His Elephant: *Irish-born keeper Pat Cronin poses with Lizzie the Indian elephant, circa 1936, in the yard of the Elephant House. Photo, a hand-painted glass slide, from Zoo Archives.*

THE PHILADELPHIA ZOOSTORY

America's first zoostory begins in earnest in the decade before the Civil War, the great divide in nineteenth-century America that separated everything into what came before and what came afterward.

Before the Civil War, Philadelphia was a bustling, prosperous young city that had just recently filled out to its adult size. The Consolidation Act of 1854 had merged the city with the six boroughs, nine districts, and thirteen townships within the 126-square-mile County of Philadelphia into one huge municipality. By a single act of the state legislature, Philadelphia became the second largest city in the United States. In fact, by 1860 with a still-swelling population of 565,529, Philadelphia ranked behind New York, London, and Paris as the fourth largest city in the Western World, roughly equal in size to Vienna, St. Petersburg, Manchester, and Liverpool.

Philadelphia had become a big city with big city problems, including poverty and lawlessness. In South Philadelphia alone there were fifty-one organized street gangs with names like the Bleeders, the Death Fetchers, and the Moyamensing Killers who marked their turf in the age-old tradition—graffiti.

The newly muscular city was also the nation's financial center, due to the continuing power of its banks. And because of the quality, number, and diversity of its factories, Philadelphia was becoming the country's preeminent manufacturing and industrial center.

CHAPTER ONE

Young Philadelphia had already amassed an impressive list of historic firsts, a list the Zoo was about to join. The city owns the bragging rights to the following firsts: paper mill (1690), life insurance company (1717), botanical garden (1728), magazine (1741), stock exchange (1754), medical school (1765), United States Congress (1790), water works (1801), college of pharmacy (1821), locomotive (1832), naval academy (1838), lager beer (1840), women's medical college (1850), and Republican National Convention (1856).

By the mid-1850s Philadelphia was a city long familiar with inventing itself and the institutions that served the social, scientific, and artistic interests of its citizens. Benjamin Franklin had founded the American Philosophical Society more than a century earlier, and it continued to serve an important role in harnessing the energy and spirit of Philadelphia's intellectual elite. Between 1812 and 1827 some of the city's most important and enduring scientific institutions were founded, including the Academy of Natural Sciences, the Pennsylvania Horticultural Society, and the Franklin Institute.

In this climate of serious scholarship and collegial associations, it was only natural that the prospect of creating a zoological society be discussed sooner or later. In the 1840s, Dr. Alfred Langdon Elwyn, a physician-philanthropist, wrote to Dr. Samuel George Morton, the pioneer of physical anthropology in America, and the president of the Academy of Natural Sciences. Dr. Elwyn was excited about the opening of the handsomely landscaped zoological garden in London's Regents Park in 1828. He suggested to Morton that invitations be sent to Philadelphia gentlemen well versed in the natural sciences and "known to be interested in the oral and mental instruction of the citizens generally" to discuss a zoo that he proposed to be built on the grounds of Lemon Hill on the east bank of the Schuylkill River overlooking what is now Boat House Row.

Elwyn's idea—or perhaps his expectation that considerable sums would be gladly donated by interested citizens—languished for more than a decade. It took the interest of Dr. William Camac, a nonpracticing "gentleman" physician who's personal fortune was the result of family land holdings in Ireland, to give the movement to create a zoo its next crucial push.

Camac was a man of many civic and scientific interests. His grandfather owned an estate in North Philadelphia named *Woodvale*, or more commonly *Camac's Woods* (Camac Street, between Twelfth and Thirteenth Streets, takes its name from the family property). After graduating with honors from Jefferson Medical College in 1852, the twenty-three-year-old became a familiar figure in the city's burgeoning community of activist citizens. Camac was a member of the Big Three—the Academy of Natural Sciences, the Franklin Institute, and the Pennsylvania Horticultural Society—and he served on a City Consolidation Committee. During his frequent trips to England and Europe, Camac visited zoos in London and Paris and returned to Philadelphia with an enthusiasm that proved contagious.

By 1859, Camac had rallied a virtual who's who of Philadelphia's most respected, wealthiest, ambitious, and powerful men to join and incorporate the Zoological Society of Philadelphia. Of the thirty-six names included in the incorporation papers, many are more familiar today as the names of schools, statues, and fountains, but the original members including George A. McCall, William M. Meredith, Morton McMichael, W. C. Swann, William Vaux,

Dr. William Camac, founder and first president of the Philadelphia Zoological Society.

Samuel Powel, Thomas Cope, Frederic Fraley, George W. Biddle, Joseph Harrison, and Samuel Merrick represented an elite of mid-nineteenth-century Philadelphia: industry, publishing, politics, science, and civic activism. Mayors, congressmen, ship-builders, scientists, and railroad presidents are included in their number. Among the thirty-six were Dr. John Leconte, one of the nation's leading naturalists, as well as John Cassin, a renown ornithologist. One charter member, Dr. William Alexander Hammond, became surgeon general of the United States. Another, coal merchant and student of paleontology, William Parker Foulke, achieved a form of immortality by having the first dinosaur skeleton discovered in the United States (in Haddonfield, New Jersey) named in his honor—Hadrosaurus Foulkei. Today, a bronze statue of that dinosaur stands just outside the doorway to the Reptile House at the Zoo.

By act of the Pennsylvania legislature on March 21, 1859, America's first zoo was born with the incorporation of the Zoological Society of Philadelphia. It is that date that establishes Philadelphia as the first zoo of any kind in the United States. The corporate seal chosen for the Society featured the head of a tiger in the middle of a circle bearing the name of the Society and the date of its incorporation (page 33). "The purpose of this corporation shall be the purchase and collection of living wild and other animals, for the purpose of public exhibition at some suitable place in the City of Philadelphia, for the instruction and recreation of the people," read the incorporation statement.

The most suitable place in Camac's view was a small parcel of ground amounting to less than a city block at the entrance to Fairmount Park where Pennsylvania Avenue meets Twenty-ninth Street. But even for so modest a venture, Camac found little public interest and even less private funding. Despite the star-studded list of names on the incorporation papers, Philadelphia greeted the idea of a zoo with a stifled yawn. "There appeared to be great apathy shown to the project," Camac would write, "and but few persons seemed to understand the objects of the society or could see the benefits to be derived."

The attack on Fort Sumter on April 15, 1861, effectively ended any further movement to establish a zoo through the conclusion of the Civil War and the immediate period of Reconstruction. During this time there was a striking change in America's (and Philadelphia's) view of itself. The Union victory led to Americans referring to their country in the singular rather than plural—"the United States *is*" replaced "the United States *are*."

By 1870 Philadelphia's population had increased by more than 50 percent. Of the 674,022 residents of Philadelphia, 27 percent were foreign born—the majority, almost 100,000, from Ireland. Discovery of oil in Western Pennsylvania led to the city becoming a major oil refining and shipping center. The Pennsylvania Railroad began its long domination of the city's business community. Philadelphia was served by forty banks, twenty-eight of them national, forty insurance companies, four savings banks, thirty-five private lending institutions, and hundreds of building and loan associations.

It was these latter that resulted in Philadelphia becoming a city of homes. Building and loan associations allowed a working-class family to live the dream of home ownership. By 1880, Philadelphia's occupancy rate was 5.7 persons per dwelling, compared to 8.25 in Boston, 8.24 in Chicago, and an incredible 16.34 in New York.

It was into this climate of a growing, confident, and comfortable city that William Camac, now a Civil War veteran, again tried to fire the eye of the tiger. In an unsigned letter published in the *North American*, Camac wrote, "There is in our city, unfortunately a great dearth of healthy forms of amusement offered to the public." He mentioned the "feeble attempts" in the past to establish a zoological garden in Philadelphia and cited the success of such facilities in foreign cities where zoos "have greater attention paid to them than any other places of recreation."

In 1872, Camac returned from a trip to Europe determined to launch a zoo in Philadelphia. Camac invited the twenty-seven surviving founders of the original thirty-six charter members of the Philadelphia Zoological Society to a meeting on April 24, 1872. Eight showed up. But they were a committed eight.

Camac was again elected president of the Society and the newly energized Board set about raising the money and finding a site for the proposed zoo.

Thanks to the delay since 1859, the original Twenty-ninth and Pennsylvania Avenue location was no longer deemed adequate. Discussions with the commissioners of Fairmount Park led to the offer of a plot of thirty-three acres on a hilly slope along the west bank of the Schuylkill immediately below the Girard Avenue Bridge, which was then under construction.

Smedley's Complete Atlas of Philadelphia in 1867, shows the area to be occupied by the Zoo bounded by Girard Avenue to the north and Thirty-fifth Street on the east. Tracks from three railroads—the Pennsylvania, Columbia, and Junction—formed the zoo's curving D-shape western boundary. The map also shows plans or existing north-south streets through the Zoo property, including Egglesfeld, Poplar, Sylvan, Penngrove, Westminster, Hutton, and Myrtle.

On the Zoo grounds was *Solitude*, the small elegant mansion built by William Penn's grandson, John Penn, on the fifteen-acre estate he purchased in 1785. Besides *Solitude*, the land to be occupied by the garden included *Spring Hill*, the estate of Ellis Yarnall, as well as farms and lots owned by George Powell, J. P. Ferree, and Samuel Powell. The Yarnalls' mansion stood at the southern end of what is now Bird Lake. The founders planned to use *Solitude* as executive offices and to turn the Yarnall mansion into a restaurant.

There was a commercial lot on the north end of the Zoo owned by the Cold Spring Ice Company, its riverside piers eventually being converted into the Zoo Landing for steamboat excursions from the city. Along the Schuylkill in the middle of the Zoo property stood a pumping station and forebay operated by the West Philadelphia (Twenty-fourth Ward) Water Works between 1855 and 1870. Just across the railroad tracks to the south of the Zoo property loomed a water tower 130 feet high and surmounted by a stat-

This circa 1870 view is the earliest-known photograph of Solitude, *owned by John Penn, grandson of William Penn. The kitchen is attached to the main house by a tunnel.*

Right: This photo from the other side of the Schuylkill River shows the West Philadelphia Water Works in operation on what later became Zoo property.

This drawing shows the ornate standpipe of the West Philadelphia Water Works, just off the Zoo property.

Solitude *houses the executive offices of the Zoo.*

Photo by John F. Anholt.

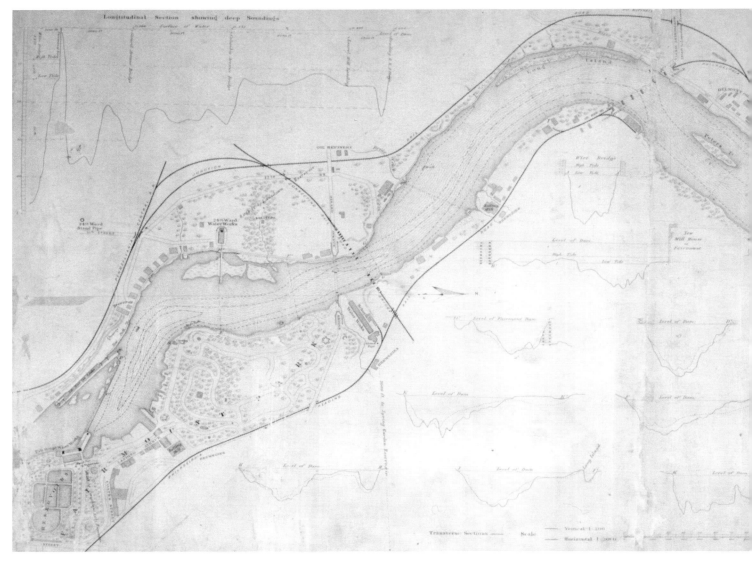

ue of George Washington. The water tower was surrounded with a masonry base and visitors could climb a spiral staircase to the top (see page 37).

A map from the 1860s shows islands in the Schuylkill River directly in front of the West Philadelphia Water Works. These islands were filled in by the Schuylkill Navigation Company, which explains why there seems to be an inordinate distance between the Water Works and the river.

In 1873 membership in the Zoological Society grew to 166, and there were weekly meetings in rent-free rooms at 35 South Third Street provided by the Westmoreland Coal Company. Despite the lack of capital, the Society managers decided to erect a high fence around the ten usable acres of zoo property (much of the land was taken up with temporary rail lines carrying material during the construction of the Girard Avenue Bridge). The new zoo was to be financed with a $150,000 loan in which shareholders

would be paid annual interest in cash and tickets. From the start, America's first zoo was a private venture, not a municipally funded enterprise. This remains a significant consideration because the Zoo's operating budget continues to be funded primarily through gate receipts rather than government subsidies.

In an appeal to potential investors in October 1873, Society Secretary John Ridgeway wrote, "The sum of $150,000 will enable the society to place the garden upon a solid and permanent basis and permit its being opened to the public in the spring of 1874, in a condition that will ensure its future prosperity and reflect credit upon the city."

Investors were to be paid dividends from the gate receipts and the shareholders were assured of the Zoo's ability to attract paying customers, at least through America's one hundredth birthday party which Philadelphia was hosting. "The millions of vis-

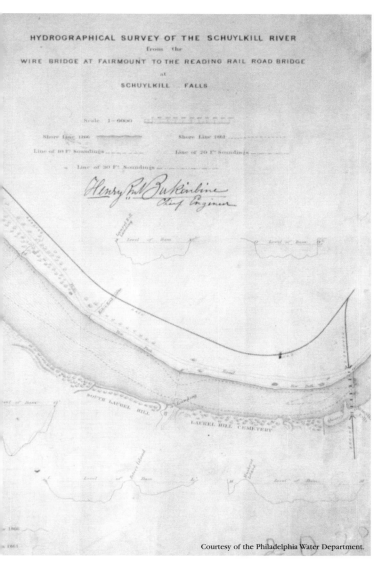

Courtesy of the Philadelphia Water Department.

This map of the Schuylkill River from the 1860s shows the area now occupied by the Zoo and the islands that existed at the time.

itors to the Centennial Exhibition, which will be located directly to the Westward will pass the north and south entrances of the Society garden, and will scarcely fail to avail themselves of the privilege of seeing its curious collection of birds, beasts and reptiles," Ridgeway wrote in his fundraising pitch. "Every endeavor is being made to place the Society in a position to profit by this influx of amusement-seeking strangers in 1876."

By March of 1874, the full amount had been raised, but not without some strings attached. Alfred Cope, a devout Quaker, offered to put up $25,000 on condition that "all malt, vinous or spirituous liquors shall be forever excluded from the premises occupied by the Society." This ban on the sale of beer and alcohol was written into the Zoo's by-laws and continues to this day.

After a dozen years of inactivity and dithering since the Zoo was incorporated in 1859, things hap-

pened fast. Herman J. Schwartzmann, a German-born engineer employed by the Fairmount Park Commission, was hired to design the Zoo. He in turn hired architects Frank Furness, George Hewitt, I. F. Chandler, Edward Collins, Charles M. Autenreith, and John Crump to design Zoo buildings. Furness, of course, has become one of Philadelphia's architectural icons. His fanciful gingerbread gate houses at the Girard Avenue Entrance remain the Zoo's signature buildings. Schwartzmann, meanwhile, would achieve his greatest fame for designing the grounds and most of the buildings of the Centennial Exhibition, including magnificent Memorial Hall.

Opening day for the Garden of the Zoological Society of Philadelphia was scheduled for July 1, 1874, whether the buildings were completed or not. The pace of construction, supervised by Board member John Vaughn Merrick, was phenomenal. Within two years, Furness's gate houses, Chandler's Monkey House and Reptile House, Hewitt's Deer House, Collins and Autenrieth's Lion and Tiger House, as well as Crump's Horse Sheds were erected.

Meanwhile Board President Camac set about the task of stocking the Zoo with animals. He wrote to noted explorer and wild animal collector Frank Thompson, then in Australia, offering him the job of zoo superintendent for a salary of $2,000 plus the use of the second floor of *Solitude* for housing. Thompson agreed and immediately set out on a collecting tour. At Camac's urging to bring back "plenty of cockatoos, parrots, flamingos," Thompson returned with a variety of colorful and exotic birds from the Southwest Pacific as well as a rare Tasmanian devil plus a number of wallabies, kangaroos, wombats, dasyures, and dingos from Australia. In fact, the Zoo's opening day collection of ten species of marsupials surpassed any total number of marsupials the garden has hosted at any one time since.

By the end of the opening year the Zoo's collection would number 616 birds, mammals, and reptiles. There was an elephant, a rhinoceros, a tiger, zebras, antelope, and six giraffes. In December of 1874 the first pair of lions and an African elephant arrived. There were, of course, prairie dogs; black, grizzly, and cinnamon bears; Canada lynx; bison; wapiti; and pronghorn antelope. The Monkey House was stocked with six species—the tufted and weeper cebus, the vervet and green monkeys, and chacma and Guinea baboons. The library in *Solitude* served as a temporary Reptile House for six snakes. The Zoo depended heavily on donations of animals. One director of the Society, Theodore L. Harrison, donated more than a hundred animals to the fledgling zoo—two snapping turtles, two common American rabbits, and 113 birds of all types. Honorary Board member Brigham Young donated two black bears which he shipped by rail from Salt Lake City. And Mrs. William Tecumseh Sherman donated a cow named Atlanta, which had accompanied her husband's march through Georgia during the Civil War.

Engraving of the original Monkey House.

HOUSE FOR MONKEYS

Carnivora House, circa 1877.

Pachyderm House.

This view of the North Gate Houses from July 1, 1874,
is the oldest-known photo of the Zoo's opening.

THE CENTENNIAL ZOOSTORY

At nine o'clock on a clear summer morning on July 1, 1874, the Garden of the Philadelphia Zoological Society opened its gates to the public and America's first zoo was officially open—finally—for business fifteen years after its founding. Three thousand inaugural visitors were greeted with flying banners, brass bands, and animals the likes of which they had never seen except in books. Admission tickets cost twenty-five cents for adults and ten cents for children, a price that would not change for fifty years. Visitors arrived by horse, carriage, boat, streetcar, and on foot. West River Drive did not exist, and the most direct route to the Zoo from the city was by steamboats which departed every fifteen minutes from a dock just above the Fairmount Dam, delivering passengers to the Zoo Landing just below the newly completed Girard Avenue Bridge, which opened to traffic on the Fourth of July three days later.

The Zoo's otherwise flawless opening day was marred by the injury of a kangaroo that ran into a fence and broke its leg after being panicked by a steam locomotive snorting around the curve of the nearby railroad tracks. A reporter with the *Philadelphia Press* observed and reported an amusing incident involving Jennie the young Indian elephant, who was chained to an oak tree in a grove near the Bear Pits. "One middle-aged maiden, seeing the beast rapidly approaching her, and supposing that it had broken loose, dropped her parasol and made a desperate effort to climb a tree," the reporter

The steamboat Undine docks at the Zoo Landing in front of the Girard Avenue Bridge in 1876.

wrote. "It was only after failing to climb the tree that the panic-stricken woman finally noticed the chain securing the elephant."

The newspaper reviews for the Zoo's opening day were glowing in both the local and out-of-town press. Philadelphians were justly proud of their newest civic attraction, and the members of the Board were relieved and delighted by the robust attendance figures. In the first eight months of operation, 227,557 people visited the Zoo, exceeding even the annual attendance of the London Zoo.

Good begat better during the second year of the zoo's operation. Attendance nearly doubled to

This old engraving depicts the original Bear Pits, built in 1874.

This newspaper engraving illustrates an event soon after opening day: A brave visitor jumped into the Bear Pits to save a little girl he thought had fallen in, but it turned out to be a doll instead.

420,000 during the Zoo's fiscal year of March 1, 1875, to March 1, 1876. The previous year's attendance record for a single day of 8,500 on July 4, 1874, was surpassed on Monday July 5, 1875, when 11,245 visitors passed through the Zoo's gates. Zoo membership was up more than 50 percent from the year before, with 770 annual members ($10 yearly) and 179 life members (a single payment of $50). The Zoo's loan total was over $250,000 with more than 400 shareholders investing the Zoo's future in return for a 6 percent annual return, plus five free single admission tickets for every $50 share.

And as good as 1875 was, the United States Centennial year promised to be even better. The globetrotting superintendent Frank J. Thompson, was replaced in April 1876 by Arthur Erwin Brown, a flinty, mustachioed herpetologist, who had been deputy superintendent of the Delaware and Raritan Canal. Although initially regarded with suspicion because of his youth and the sudden replacement of the popular Thompson, twenty-six-year-old Brown quickly earned the confidence of the staff and city's sometimes contentious scientific community and he began the long tradition of multidecade service by the zoo's superintendents, keepers, curators, gardeners, pathologists, and other employees. Brown's tenure as superintendent extended for thirty-four years, from 1876 to 1910 when he was felled by a heart attack while at work in the garden at the age of sixty.

Philadelphia had been preparing for the America's one hundredth birthday celebration since it won approval by the United States Centennial Commission in 1871 to host a six-month-long world's fair in Fairmount Park to commemorate American independence. In terms of tourism and convention business this was the equivalent of scoring the Super Bowl, the World Series, every major league professional sports All-Star Games and *both* the Republican and Democratic National Conventions in a single year. And the Philadelphia Zoo stood ready to reap its share of "amusement-seeking strangers."

North Entrance to the Zoo on Girard Avenue, circa 1876. Lemon Hill Observation Tower, built for the U.S. Centennial Exhibition, is in the background.

On May 10, President Ulysses S. Grant and Emperor Dom Pedro of Brazil opened the Centennial Exhibition by throwing the switch that started the giant Corliss Engine in Machinery Hall just below where the Mann Center for the Performing Arts stands today. The massive two-cylinder engine, with its forty-four-inch-wide pistons, and ten-foot stroke, turned a massive fifty-six-ton flywheel measuring thirty feet in diameter. This single engine powered the other eight hundred machines in display from around the world.

American curassows, crested game birds that the Grants had donated to the zoo a few months earlier.

The millions of visitors expected for the duration of the Centennial Exhibition did not materialize in the early months of its run, primarily because of a heat wave that struck in mid-June and lasted through July, with temperatures reaching one hundred degrees ten days in a row. In fact, the Zoo's attendance dropped for the first six months of 1876 over the year before. But then the paralyzing heat broke

The Girard Avenue Entrance, at left in 1876, is dwarfed by the Girard Avenue Bridge, then newly built and said to be the widest bridge in the world. Girard College is behind that. The building to the right is a "parking lot" for horse-drawn carriages.

Following the opening ceremony, the President and Mrs. Grant strolled down Girard Avenue to promenade along the new bridge, then said to be the widest bridge in the world. Afterward, the First Family toured the Zoo and sought out the pair of South

in August and attendance increased by 2,817 over the previous August. In September the increase in attendance leaped to 65,389. In October it reached an incredible 154,800 increase over the previous year. On Sunday, October 29, the Zoo attracted an astounding 20,715 visitors, a single-day attendance record that would not be broken for seventy-five years. November saw another increase of 49,999 and those attendance figures were mirrored by the crowds at the Centennial Grounds just a few blocks away where the autumn surge in visitors exceeded all expectations. The final tally for the six months of

Patrons enjoy themselves at the original Zoo Restaurant in this old engraving.

This early vintage Zoo illustration shows a keeper putting horse blankets on the giraffes.

the Centennial Exhibition was 10,164,489. The Zoo's attendance topped 657,000, an increase of 237,519 over the year before. It would be decades and decades, and two world wars before the Zoo would again enjoy such numbers of visitors.

During those lusty early years, the Zoo took in considerably more money than it spent. Salaries for the first year totaled $11,155. That figure jumped to $21,183 in 1875 and topped off at $24,343 in the Centennial year. Another remarkable budget item during those first few happy years romping in the garden was the relatively large expenditure for music, presumably for brass bands to serenade visitors. The music budget for the first year was $1,997. The following year it reached $3,521. In 1876 the Zoo spent $5,259 on music, compared with $4,896 for advertising.

Clearly something was bound to give. And it did in 1877: the year the music died.

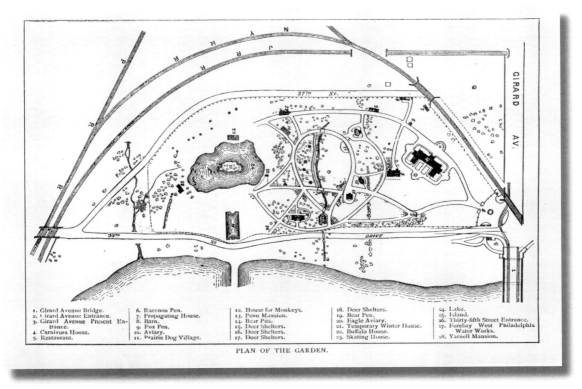

1. Girard Avenue Bridge.	6. Raccoon Pen.	12. House for Monkeys.	18. Deer Shelters.	24. Lake.
2. Girard Avenue Entrance.	7. Propagating House.	13. Penn Mansion.	19. Bear Pen.	25. Island.
3. Girard Avenue Present Entrance.	8. Barn.	14. Bear Pits.	20. Eagle Aviary.	26. Thirty-fifth Street Entrance.
4. Carnivora House.	9. Fox Pen.	15. Deer Shelters.	21. Temporary Winter House.	27. Forebay West Philadelphia Water Works.
5. Restaurant.	10. Aviary.	16. Deer Shelters.	22. Buffalo House.	28. Yarnell Mansion.
	11. Prairie Dog Village.	17. Deer Shelters.	23. Skating House.	

PLAN OF THE GARDEN.

In this 1875 plan, the street in front of the Zoo was named Thirty-fifth Street.

Zoo visitors stroll hand in hand near the Lion House, circa 1876.

Original Stars:
Pompeii and Bolivar

When the Zoo opened its doors for the first time on July 1, 1874, there were some notable species missing from the collection. No lions . . . no tigers . . . but bears! Oh my! The first pair of lions arrived in December of 1874, the male of which was named Pompeii. For most Philadelphians, Pompeii was the first King of Beasts they'd ever seen, and he enjoyed a certain celebrity which was immortalized by a series of paintings by Henry Ossawa Tanner. Tanner, the son of a runaway slave who became a learned theologian, was a brilliant artist who studied under Thomas Eakins at the Pennsylvania Academy of Fine Arts. In the late 1870s and early 1880s, Tanner spent hundreds of hours at the Zoo drawing anatomical studies of animals. (His art school descendents can be seen almost any day with sketchpads in hand.) Clearly the young artist was drawn to the noble visage of Pompeii, who was featured in no fewer than three of Tanner's paintings between 1880 and 1886—*Lion at Home*, *Lion Licking Its Paw*, and if anyone was wondering which lion he was painting, *Pomp at the Zoo*. Tanner moved to Paris, where he found his race less of an impediment to his success as a painter. Pompeii lived out his days at the Philadelphia Zoo, where he died in 1884.

The first rhinoceros at the Zoo was named Pete. He was a massive Indian rhino that the Zoo purchased from Barnum's Circus in 1875. Pete lived for more than a quarter century, and upon his death in 1901 his body was mounted and placed on display in the Academy of Natural Sciences for decades.

In its entire history, the Zoo has only owned three male Indian elephants, and the first was the largest of all. Bolivar was his name. He stood ten feet tall at the shoulder and weighed twelve thousand pounds, roughly two tons more than the Zoo's largest elephant today. Like most male elephants, Bolivar was temperamental and capable of carnage. Even though he was credited with killing two handlers during his twenty-seven years with the Adam Fourpagh Circus, the Zoo accepted the donation of the elephant in 1888. Fourpaugh himself triumphantly marched Bolivar into the Zoo on Christmas Day of that year. Stay-at-home zoo life suited the massive bull elephant. He lived out his days without attacking any of his keepers or visitors and he died of old age on July 31, 1908. Like Pete the rhino, Bolivar ended up at the Academy of Natural Sciences, where his skeleton was mounted in the entrance hall. The bones of Bolivar's rib cage were so wide that members of the Zoo Board once ate dinner at a table set beneath his skeleton.

Pompeii was king of the Zoo in 1880, but Merlin rules in 1999. He even looks like a wizard.

Pompeii the Lion, *circa 1880.*
Henry Ossawa Tanner, then
a student of Thomas Eakins,
painted portraits of Pompeii
several times. One was called
Pomp at the Zoo.

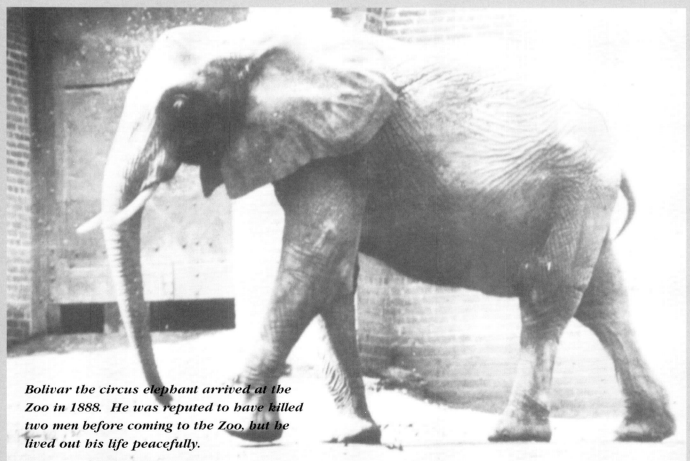

Bolivar the circus elephant arrived at the
Zoo in 1888. He was reputed to have killed
two men before coming to the Zoo, but he
lived out his life peacefully.

This charming view of the garden was photographed in the 1890s. The bridge crosses over the Beaver Pond.

AFTER THE HONEYMOON ZOOSTORY

The splendid zoological garden at Fairmount Park, Philadelphia, was opened to the public July 1, 1874, yet it has the air and general appearance of long-established like institutions in Europe. Its collection of animals is already very extensive, lacking hardly anything of grand importance to the mass of patrons, unless we might mention the hippopotamus.

—Harper's New Monthly Magazine, April 18, 1879

By the time *Harper's* praised the Philadelphia Zoo in a feature article five years after opening day, the Zoo's collection of animals had increased to 1,008. But by then there was something else lacking to the mass of patrons besides the hippo. What was lacking was, well, a mass of patrons.

The Centennial year of 1876 set a standard of Zoo attendance that would not be met again until after World War II. From a record high of 657,295 admissions in 1876, Zoo attendance plummeted to 203,773. That was an astonishing decrease of 453,522 visitors in a single year. At the sixth annual meeting of the Zoological Society of Philadelphia in April 1878, the grim figures were read to the members from the Annual Report showing a deficit of almost $20,000 in a total budget of less that $80,000. Drastic economy measures were instituted. The food budget alone was cut by 80 percent by the Zoo's decision to feed the carnivores horse meat from older animals purchased on the hoof from the U.S. Cavalry. Gone—vanished—were the annual expenditures for "music" that had reached $5,259 the year before. Gone too was the Zoo's annual payroll that had risen each of the Zoo's first three years to a total of $24,343 during the Centennial. In 1877 Zoo salaries were slashed to $20,416. In 1878 the Zoo payroll totaled a mere $16,720. In a period of two years, the Philadelphia Zoo had gone from toast of the town to plain old toast.

"My experiences as Prosector of the Zoological Society convince me that during the first six months of the existence of the garden, the principal causes of death were three: (1) Improper food in both quantity and quality; (2) Effects of temperature; (3) Ill-constructed cages, wanting in sufficient space and deficient in the necessary appurtenances, such as water to bathe in, trees to climb, soil to burrow in, etc., accord-

Antelope House, designed in 1877, is the only original animal exhibit building still standing.

Or so it seemed. Ironically, the Zoo began to make its greatest contributions to the world of science during what would prove to be a long period of seeming public disinterest. From the very beginning, the Zoo kept careful records of the causes of death of every animal in the collection. Animal autopsies, called necropsies, were conducted (and still are) by the zoo pathologist, called a prosector in the 1870s.

ing to the nature of the animal," reported Henry C. Chapman in his first prosector's report to Zoo directors in 1876. In that report, Chapman revealed, without specifically noting, that the leading cause of death in monkeys was tuberculosis. The significance of this would later lead the Zoo to become a pioneer in protective quarantine of primates and the use of glass rather than bars to separate animals from visitors.

Original Monkey House, 1874–1898.

What Chapman learned from these animal autopsies, led to immediate changes in diet and living conditions that considerably reduced the mortality among animals in the collection. But he never lost sight of the ultimate paradox, and wrote in 1877: "When we consider the unnatural conditions to which an animal is subjected under confinement and the exigencies of a menagerie often unavoidably demand, the wonder is not that the animals die but that they live."

For the next twenty years, the Zoo's attendance fluctuated annually from the low to high 200,000s. Zoo founder William Camac stepped down as president in 1878, and left the Zoo Board the following year. A few years later he took his family on a boat trip up the Nile, leaving his business affairs in the hands of a friend who promptly embezzled his way

through the family fortune. Camac returned to Philadelphia, penniless, and moved to New York where he died in 1899 at the age of seventy. "Today, he is nearly unknown in the city," wrote John Sedgewick about Camac in the 1986 book *The Peaceable Kingdom.* "The situation is little better at the Zoo. His portrait hangs with those of the rest of the directors along one corridor of the administration building, but otherwise there is no memorial. None of the buildings are named after him; no sculpture of him adorns the grounds. At the zoo he founded, he is a forgotten man."

The 1880s were a period of continuing growth in the animal collection—the Zoo finally got that hippo *Harper's* wrote about—and attempts were made to attract visitors and increase revenue by offering elephant rides in a howdah mounted on the back of

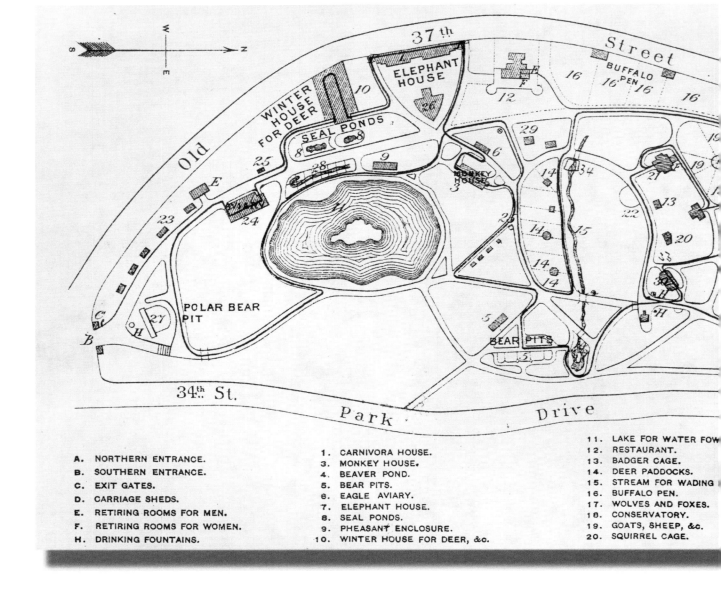

Josephine, the Indian elephant. Still Zoo attendance remained as sluggish as the economy. At twenty-five cents, the price of admission was formidable to, say, Philadelphia policemen, who in 1884 earned $2.38 a day. The average annual salary for a factory worker during that time was $500, with skilled machinists at the Baldwin Locomotive Works pushing the earnings envelope at $605 per year, while textile workers lagged behind at $355. Do the math—there wasn't a lot of discretionary income for family outings.

At the general membership meeting in 1885 the sorry state of affairs was laid out. The number of dues-paying members to the Society had dropped to 350 from well over a thousand a few years before. The Zoo's desperate financial straits were described in detail, and although $22,000 was raised on the spot to meet the budget shortfall, the Board warned in a statement to the press, "that nothing but a large

endowment will ensure the permanency of the garden. Until then the existence of the society will always be uncertain and sometimes precarious."

As bad at the eighties were, the not-so-gay nineties were worse. In the beginning of the decade the Zoo lowered the price of admission to ten cents for adults and five cents for children on Saturdays and legal holidays (except the Fourth of July). A year later the Zoo entered into its longstanding relationship with the Philadelphia public schools by providing ten thousand free tickets to schoolchildren. The passage of the Compulsory School Attendance Act in 1895 would increase the number of public students to 153,000 by the end of the decade. Despite such attendance boosting efforts admissions to the garden plummeted by 52,000 in 1892. The Board noted in the Annual Report that this precipitous decline had caused "anxious questioning whether the garden has

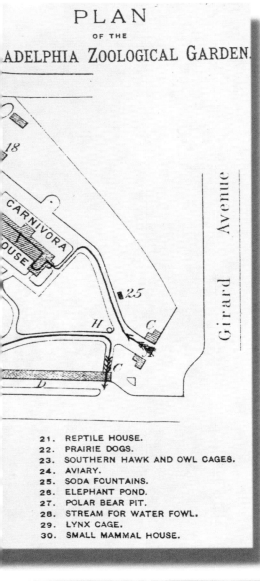

PLAN
OF THE
ADELPHIA ZOOLOGICAL GARDEN

Girard Avenue

CARNIVORA HOUSE

21. REPTILE HOUSE.
22. PRAIRIE DOGS.
23. SOUTHERN HAWK AND OWL CAGES.
24. AVIARY.
25. SODA FOUNTAINS.
26. ELEPHANT POND.
27. POLAR BEAR PIT.
28. STREAM FOR WATER FOWL.
29. LYNX CAGE.
30. SMALL MAMMAL HOUSE.

In 1889, Thirty-fifth Street became Thirty-fourth Street when a bridge over the train tracks linked it to Thirty-fourth Street. Old Thirty-seventh Street is now called Zoological Drive.

become in some measure a victim of popular apathy." The following year attendance dropped another 18,762. "The previous year was such a marked depression in affairs that comparison of the receipts does not fully indicate the serious conditions which it has been necessary for your board to meet," read the Annual Report for 1893. "The present year was entered into with the knowledge that it was the most critical period in the history of the society."

The collapse of Philadelphian Jay Cooke's financial empire triggered the nationwide business slump known as the Panic of 1893 (think of a Panic as a Recession with the heebie-jeebies). It would mark the last time a single Philadelphia financial institution wielded such influence over the nation's economy. And it placed the Zoo on the precipice.

In that year City Council came to the rescue with an appropriation of $10,000. The Board noted the Council's generosity: "In the opinion of the Board, this liberal and broad-minded action has alone prevented the closing of the Garden and the dispersal of the collection." But even this cash windfall did not prevent more belt tightening, or as the Annual Report stated, "measures of economy so stringent as to be permissible only as temporary expedients." In his superintendent's report, Arthur Brown described how

This circa 1893 aerial view shows the Zoo's Big D configuration with Center City in the background.

the lack of funds "has required a postponement even of urgently needed repairs."

In 1894 attendance dropped another 14,840. An average of 550 people were visiting the Zoo each day generating average daily gate receipts of $76.58 for the entire Zoo. "It may be regarded as certain that conditions more generally unfavorable to the financial prosperity of the Society have never existed than during this past year." The following year saw an actual boost in attendance by almost 3,000 and the Board expressed the hope that the modest increase "may be regarded as the beginning of a return to a condition in which receipts will more nearly balance the cost of maintenance."

In 1896, the year after the first increase in attendance in a decade, admissions went into a free-fall dropping by more than 30,000. Part of the cause was the number of the Zoo's potential visitors who were now filling streetcars flocking to the newly opened amusement parks in Willow Grove and nearby Woodside Park. "There is a disadvantage in competing for popular support with the many resorts able to offer striking and varied novelties," Superintendent Brown wrote. Twenty years after the fabulous Centennial year, Brown noted "receipts from admissions reached a lower point than any previous year since the opening of the garden." Brown pointed out that "the present cost of operating the garden is no greater than it was 20 years ago. . . . Indeed it is not easy to say where the practice of economy could be further applied."

City Council increased is appropriation to $15,000 that year, which the Board described, in the purplest of prose, as "maybe the cheapest and most effective means of preserving to Philadelphia one of its public institutions whose popularity is undoubtedly great and which belongs in a class, by consent of all nations, filling a necessary place among educational and diverting influences of human society."

And it only got worse. The 1890s ended with the Zoo losing another 21,000 in attendance from the year before. Total attendance in 1898–99 was 153,016—an average of 416 visitors a day, generating income of a paltry $56.63 per day. "Whatever may be the cause of the deficiency, the dependence of the existence of the Garden upon the appropriation made by City Council becomes each year more apparent." And if 1898 wasn't bad enough already, an early morning fire destroyed the Zoo Restaurant on October 20.

Psychologically, the Zoo had reached its lowest ebb, a spiritual depression that would not be matched again until another fire struck nearly a century later.

Ape and Monkey House, designed in 1896.

Monkey House exterior cages, designed in 1896.

Old Bear Pits.

Aviary outdoor cages.

Giraffes take their name from the Arabic zarafa, *although they were also known as camelopards— a combined camel and leopard.*

It takes a lot of men to measure an anaconda, which is Sinhalese for "lightning stem."

Copyright © Tom Hartman.

What's in a Name?

The word **orangutan** means "man of the forest" in the Malay language, which is the language spoken by the people who are most likely to run into an *oran utan* in their neck of the jungle on the islands of Sumatra and Borneo. Generally speaking, though, most of the animals we are truly familiar with take their names the old-fashioned way—through continuing corruption of various ancient tongues over the centuries, including Latin, Greek and Sanskrit.

Gorilla, for instance is from the Greek *gorillai* which translates into "a tribe of hairy women," which is exactly what Hanno, the Carthaginian navigator, thought gorillas were when he first spotted them on land as he sailed off the west coast of Africa in the fifth century B.C. **Monkey** is another word that takes its meaning from a specific yet obscure origin. My dictionary says **monkey** comes from the Middle Low German proper name *Moneke* which is the name of the son of Martin the Ape, in the medieval beast epic *Reynard the Fox.* You could look it up.

It may be a pygmy marmoset, but it still means "grotesque figure" in French.

You could also look up **lemur**, which comes from the Latin word for "ghost" or "specter"; **marmoset**, which comes from the Old French for "grotesque figure," or **chimpanzee**, which is the French version of the native Bantu word *kampenzi.* French, Spanish, and Portuguese explorers or colonists gave many animals their names, sometimes by adopting the indigenous population's name for an animal, such as **giraffe**, which is French for the Arabic *zarafa*, or by simply describing what the animal looked like, such as the **armadillo**, which means "little armored creature" in Spanish.

You'd never guess that **chameleon** means "earth lion" in Greek, or that **anaconda** is Sinhalese for "lightning stem," or that **camel** could be Latin *camelus* or Greek *kamelos*, or that **alligator** is Spanish for lizard, *el lagorto.* And leave it to the French to say **antelope** when they mean "a fabulous horned animal."

English has it fair share of animal names, even some that don't sound English, like **salamander**, which is Middle English for "a mythological reptile that lives in fire," *salamandre.* **Badger** is also Middle English from the badge of white on the animal's face. **Bear** is Old English for "brown animal." **Dove** is Middle English for "dull." **Frog** is Middle English, by way of Sanskrit, for the word meaning "hops" or "jumps." And **sloth** is Middle English for "slow."

Lion is Latin from *Leo.* **Tiger** is a little bit of everything—Old English, Old French, Greek, Latin, even Iranian for *tigra* meaning "sharp." **Baboon** is Old French for "ape" or "fool." **Macaque** is Portuguese for "monkey." **Bison** is Latin for "wild ox." **Elephant** is Greek for "ivory." **Rhinoceros** is also Greek for "nose horned." And **ibis** is Egyptian for "sacred bird."

Native tongues from animals in the new world give us names like **raccoon**, which is from the Algonquin word *aroughcun.* **Tanager** is from the South American Tupi *tangara* for "bird."

Budgerigar is native-Australian aborigine for "parrot." **Capybara** is Tupi *kapigivara* for "one who eats grass." **Tapir** is Tupi *tapyra* for "large mammal." And **skunk** comes from the Eastern Algonquin *segogw*, although **skink** comes from the Greek *skinkos*.

Langur is Hindi for "having a tail" and **cheetah** is Hindi for "leopard." **Caracal** is Turkish for "black ear." **Buffalo** is Italian for "wild ox." **Goose**, on the other hand is Old Norse for "gas," which my dictionary suggests, "probably because geese sometimes attack children from the rear." Are you keeping up with this?

Echidna is either Latin for "viper, adder" or German for "leech."

Blesbok is Afrikaans for "blaze buck" with blaze meaning "a light colored spot on the animals face."

Dromedary is Greek for *dromas* meaning "a runner," which is what dromedaries were—fast camels. **Eagle** is Latin for "eagle." **Boa** is Latin for "large water serpent" and **lizard** is Latin for "leg" or "limb."

Would you believe that **flamenco** is Spanish for "flame"? Of course, you would.

And if you were eighteenth-century British explorer Captain James Cook you might believe the name given to an odd-looking creature that moved on all four like a fur-covered Slinky or hopped on two legs like a rabbit. "Ka-n-gar-oo" said the aborigine in Queensland, Australia, in response to Captain Cook's repeated question "What do you call that animal?" But as the story Down Under goes, in that aboriginal tongue the word **kangaroo** had another meaning: "I don't understand what you're saying."

Red kangaroo.

A parent eagle flys back to its eaglets in the nest.

In any language the word skunk means one thing.

Goat rides in the Zoo, circa 1907.

INTO THE TWENTIETH CENTURY

The new century marked the arrival of better times at the Zoo and an explosion in Philadelphia's population. Between 1900 and 1915 the city's population increased by almost 400,000—from 1,293,000 to 1,684,000. It was unprecedented, the single largest population boom in a similar span of years in the city's history. Newcomers included immigrants from Russia (95,744 according to the 1920 census), Poland (31,122), and Italy (63,223) which together now made up a third of Philadelphia's foreign-born population. The city's black population would more than double during the first two decades of the century, from 63,000 to 134,000.

Such rapid growth placed extraordinary demands on the city's government to provide public services—rapid transit, gas, electric, most of which were privately owned. It also created irresistible opportunities for corrupt politicians to feather their own nests in the awarding of public contracts. Such officially sanctioned corruption was not lost on either the local or national press. In 1903 muckraker Lincoln Steffens labeled Philadelphia "the worst governed city in the United States." In 1904 an editorial in the *Philadelphia North American* referred to City Hall's entrenched Republican administration as "the confederation of evil that rules the city." At the same time, Philadelphia was earning a reputation for smug acceptance of the status quo—"corrupt and contented" Steffens called it. "The one thing unforgivable in Philadelphia," wrote *Harper's Magazine* in

Ape and Monkey House, designed in 1896.

1916, "is to be new, to be different from what has been."

At America's first zoo, however, new and different was the order of the day. In the few decades since its founding, the Philadelphia Zoo had established new standards of animal husbandry and diet through constant scientific study. Experiments in the effects of cooler temperatures on tropical animals revealed that many thrived on the fresh winter air. Monkeys were placed in moveable cages and rolled outside for periods each day, even in subfreezing weather. During the winter, temperature in buildings housing the lions, tigers, elephants, and antelope was allowed to drop into the low forties. The animals not only demonstrated no ill effects, but they remained remarkably free from disease. Superintendent Arthur Brown, no doubt pleased by the lower heating bills, suggested radical changes in the routine year-round care of many exotic animals.

In 1904, the Zoo's Laboratory of Comparative Pathology that would later be named in honor of pathologist Dr. Charles B. Penrose, opened under the direction of Dr. C. Y. White. Until then, necropsies had been performed off Zoo property at the University of Pennsylvania's Pepper Clinical Laboratory. It was here that much pioneering work in the study of the cause and prevention of tuberculosis in primates was accomplished. In 1902, a total of twenty-three monkeys died of tuberculosis many of which had given no symptoms and seemed "even to appear in fairly good health until within a few days or hours of death. In many cases they seemed as active and well as their healthy companions." In 1903, thirty-six monkeys died of TB. In 1904 another thirty-six. In 1905 a total of thirty-nine monkeys and fourteen lemurs died of the disease. During this period, the Zoo established protocols for quarantine of arriving monkeys and other primates especially susceptible to tuberculosis. Under the direction of Dr. Penrose, Dr. Ellen P. Corson-White, then the highest-ranking

Interior of Ape and Monkey House.

woman to work for the Zoo, and Dr. Herbert Fox developed a tuberculin test that would eventually be used worldwide on both human and animals. The discovery that primates were so susceptible to TB infection from human contact led to the installation of glass partitions in exhibition areas between the monkeys and human visitors. (Ironically, this attempt to protect the animals from the public backfired years later when some of the workmen who installed the glass were infected with TB. An epidemic broke out that eventually killed half the Zoo's collection of monkeys in 1931. The Ape and Monkey House was closed to the public for a month and a half, while the surviving animals were quarantined and tested repeatedly for signs of TB. Upon reopening, not another case of TB was recorded at the Ape and Monkey House until its demolition in 1984.)

The necropsies performed at the lab continued to show how poor diet effected mortality. "Many of the losses during the year may be attributed to the desire of the average visitors to feed the animals," read the pathologist report of 1907, "and while it may be checked to some extent, the practice is, unfortunately, impossible to prevent altogether." During the next three decades, the Zoo's success in nutritional research would have an international impact on the zoo world.

Attendance at the garden during the early 1900s rebounded from the low of 153,016 in 1898, reaching 233,604 in 1904 before gradually dipping to 171,577 in 1910, the year Superintendent Arthur Brown died suddenly at the age of sixty. In his thirty-four years at the helm of the zoo, only the first two could be considered a financial success. "They represented the great Centennial exhibition, which centered the attention of the world upon Philadelphia," read the memo-

rial to Brown, published in that year's Annual Report. The memorial attempted to rationalize the Zoo's thirty-plus years of faltering attendance and hand-to-mouth financing since those halcyon days of 1876. "While this city developed more and more into a manufacturing center, New York became the great metropolis of the East, attracting visitors from all over the country. For these reasons the receipts, as shown by our accounts, demonstrated shortly after his work began the difficulty of the task our new superintendent had to contend with."

The task was now passed to a new superintendent, Brown's longtime assistant Robert D. Carson, who served for seven years of up and down attendance and a steadily increasing budget thanks in great part to City Council appropriations that increased from $30,000 annually in 1909 to $50,000 annually in to 1912. When Carson took over the post the Zoo's annual expenditures were $61,407, including $24,605 in salaries—almost the same amount as was spent by the Zoo in 1876. By 1917 annual expenditures had raised each year to a total of $104,274 and such yearly increases continued until the stock market crash of 1929, the year the Zoo's budget reached $229,227 (only to be slashed to $134,022 in 1932 during the darkest days of the Great Depression).

During World War I, the Zoo prospered under the direction of the new superintendent—another man named Brown—C. Emerson Brown. In 1917 and 1918 Zoo attendance increased by more than one hundred thousand and the Zoo's annual salary payroll reached $36,000. The Zoo was learning a lesson about spending money to increase attendance, as Philadelphia's wartime economy boomed. In South Philadelphia the opening of the world's largest shipyard at Hog Island in 1917 employed thirty thousand skilled and

unskilled workers. And in North Philadelphia thousands were employed at the ten-story Ford Motor Company factory at Broad and Lehigh where all the steel helmets worn by American soldiers were manufactured.

Instead of a postwar slump, the Zoo's attendance continued to zoom from 299,091 in 1918 to 371,256 in 1919 and to 455,416 in 1920, despite the cost of admission being raised from twenty-five to thirty-five cents for adults and from ten to fifteen cents for children on June 1, 1920. The decade of the 1920s saw the number of Zoo visitors never dip below 300,000. Attendance reached a decade high of 477,123 in 1927, one year after the introduction of a quarterly publication for the Zoo members called *Bulletin of the Philadelphia Zoological Society*, the first nonscientific or financial report published by the Society. The *Bulletin*, and its succeeding in-house publications: *The Philadelphia Zoo, Fauna, America's First Zoo*, and *ZooOne* were, and are, an invaluable source of Zoo lore and archival photographs.

Vol. 1, No. 1 of the *Bulletin* for April and May of 1926 shows the Zoo's temporary exhibit at the Sesquicentennial Exhibition grounds in South Philadelphia in what is now the sports stadium com-

Bird House interior, flying enclosure.

plex above the Navy Yard. On display was the Zoo's reigning male lion Sultan, as well as a buffalo, a bald eagle, and grizzly bear named Sesqui. The Zoo had placed high hopes on an anticipated windfall of visitors drawn to Philadelphia during the celebration of the nation's 150th birthday, but in fact Zoo attendance for 1926 was the second lowest of the decade—312,901. Rain fell on 107 of the 184 days the Sesquicentennial was opened and the exhibition never drew the crowds expected by organizers.

During the 1920s the Zoo set longevity records for a number of animals that previously had never survived long in captivity. Among them were the reclusive echidna, which had survived for more than twenty years at the Zoo on a daily diet consisting of one egg and one pint of milk placed in separate pans inside its cage. The public rarely saw this creature

because the nocturnal echidna spent its days sleeping in a dark box in its cage, but the *Bulletin* noted, "Any of our members wishing to see this animal may have the box-lid lifted upon request to the keeper." Another longevity record holder was Bobby, a white-handed gibbon, who marked his twenty-first year at the Zoo on July 26, 1927. At the time it was rare for gibbons to survive more than four years in captivity, and the Zoo credited his health to the relatively infection-free glass cage he had inhabited in the Small Mammal House since his arrival. That and his diet of orange slices, tapioca, bananas, rice, bread and "milk with a little lime water in it." The celebration of Bobby's longevity (he would live another ten years) coincided with the arrival of a baby gorilla who was destined to become the most famous animal at America's first zoo. His name was Bamboo.

This was a good era for the Zoo. Attendance was up and the collection was growing with the addition

Gorilla Bamboo, aged about one year, with C. Emerson Brown, director of the Zoo, on the day of Bamboo's arrival, August 5, 1927.

Lion House.

Lion House interior.

of significant animals that enhanced the Zoo's reputation. On May 25, 1928, a giant Aldabra tortoise joined three Galapagos tortoises acquired earlier that year. The Aldabra, the Zoo *Bulletin* noted, was "probably the last one obtainable because they are becoming so scarce the government is refusing permits to take more." (Those tortoises, incidentally, are alive and well living in the Reptile House—the Zoo's oldest animals.) A three-year-old Siberian tiger was donated to the Zoo by an anonymous patron, who was clearly not a University of Pennsylvania alumnus based on the name the donor insisted be given to his orange-and-black-furred gift—Princeton.

On September 25, 1928, the Zoo celebrated the birth of Lucky, the first baby orangutan to be born in the United States. Less than a week later the first chimpanzee bred in captivity was born at the Zoo. His name was Julius, and with his birth the Zoo's primate collection numbered fifteen—four gibbons, six chimps, four orangutans, and one gorilla. "Never in

the history of this garden," wrote Superintendent C. Emerson Brown, "nor any other in the United States at least, has there been such an imposing array of anthropoids exhibited at one time." Another Zoo milestone was marked in 1928 with the installation of electricity. On July 27 at 1:00 p.m. a switch was thrown "and all buildings were flooded with light for the first time in the history of the garden." (Although not for the first time in the city—electric lights had been in use for almost forty years in some Center City office buildings.)

In 1929, Zoo Board Vice President Arthur Sewell presented the Zoo with six electric eels which were moved to a large aquarium near the main entrance of the Reptile House. One of the specimens was six feet long and could generate enough of an electric jolt to "knock a horse down or temporarily paralyze a man." The electric eels arrived in the same year as the stock market crash that knocked America down and came close to paralyzing America's first zoo permanently.

Original Reptile House.

Bison graze on what is now the Impala Lawn in front of the old Lion House.

A Zoo pathway beckons.

*Below:
Hoofstock were
housed in rustic
wooden structures
arranged in a circle.
Even today, keepers
refer to "the circle."*

Star Stories:
Bamboo and Massa

All things being equal, some animals are more valuable to the Zoo than others. Call it human nature, but people like cuddly better than not cuddly. Scary better than not scary. Mammalian better than reptilian. Loud better than quiet. Active better than passive. Human-like better than nonhuman-like. For those reasons, the star animals at the Zoo—or at least, the animals people came to see over and other again during the past century-plus—have usually possessed one or more of those traits in abundance. And what could have more star power than a cuddly, scary, loud, active human-like mammal? Bamboo was his name. His entire name could have been Bamboo-at-the-zoo because that's how people spoke of the first gorilla in America's first zoo, the first gorilla to survive more than a year anywhere in the United States.

Bamboo, February 1939.

Bamboo was an infant when he arrived at the Zoo inside a suitcase—literally—on August 5, 1927. Traveling with him in an accompanying suitcase was his future cagemate, Lizzie the chimpanzee, who became his constant companion and roughhousing antagonist until Bamboo grew too large and powerful. As a baby Bamboo was cared for by head keeper Jim McCrossen virtually from dawn until dusk. When McCrossen was struck and killed by a speeding car on Girard Avenue one evening when heading home from work in 1931 after fifty-one years at the Zoo, no other keeper could control the increasingly irascible ape. Bamboo, who grew to be an impressive six feet tall, 435 pounds, took pleasure in abusing his keepers, the public, and any other humans he could get close enough to throw something at, or better yet, touch. Especially press photographers. On March 30, 1934, the *Evening Ledger* explained, "The reason there is no recent photo of Bamboo, the zoo's gorilla, is because the photographer has a fondness for his head. Every time he goes near Bamboo's cage to get a picture, Bamboo throws things. All sorts of thing." Bamboo was lightning quick and could snatch a hat off anyone foolish enough to lean too close to his cage. "He once had the largest collection of crushed straw hats in the country," the *Evening Ledger* reported, "and the zoo had the longest list of complaints."

It was not always humorous. In 1947 the door to Bamboo's outdoor enclosure was unlocked while veteran Monkey House keeper Ralph Davis was inside the gorilla's cage cleaning up. It was a mistake that nearly cost the keeper his life. Bamboo grabbed Davis, bit him severely and dragged him out of the open cage door into the outer yard. Other keepers distracted the gorilla,

Photo by Newton Hartman.

Gorilla Bamboo and chimpanzee Lizzie with Keeper Jim McCrosson soon after their arrival in 1927.

he broke out into the main Zoo, but the gorilla never tested the flimsy fence. Keepers tried to coax him back into his cage with food, tried to scare him with live snakes—gorillas *hate* snakes—but what finally did the trick was a spray of water from a fire hose. Bamboo retreated inside and eventually ambled back inside his cage.

Bamboo's reputation grew with each passing year. He was the oldest gorilla in captivity for most of his thirty-three years at the Zoo. "The most interesting and worthwhile object or person I have ever seen in Philadelphia," wrote Harvard anthropologist Earnest A. Hooton, "was a gorilla named Bamboo at the Philadelphia Zoo." During the Korean War, an Intelligence and Reconnaissance (I&R) Platoon in the 187th Airborne wrote to the Zoo asking for a pin-up photo of Bamboo. "It is our pleasure to inform you that you have been voted Mister I&R of 1952, 'The boy we would most like to have with us out on combat patrol.' Would you please send us a snapshot that we can hang in our bunker." When Bamboo died of a heart attack in 1961, his obit in *America's First Zoo* magazine began, "He was mean, treacherous, and unlovely . . . but Bamboo, the elderly gorilla that had been the Zoo's leading animal citizen for more than thirty-three years, died amidst a widespread feeling of regret, shared by thousands of fans who watched him grow up in the Philadelphia Zoo."

allowing Davis to escape with a broken shoulder and severe head lacerations, but Bamboo was now running up and down outside his cage. The only thing preventing him from rampaging through the Zoo was a fine wire-mesh fence designed to stop people from throwing food into the cages. Three Zoo employees with high powered rifles took up positions to shoot Bamboo if

Massa, March 1940.

knocked over the bucket of water, startling the young gorilla, who attacked his mistress, severing an artery in her arm with his teeth and nearly killing her if it hadn't been for a houseguest who whacked Massa over the head with an iron skillet.

Mrs. Lintz sold Massa to the Zoo for $6,000 in December 1935. The Zoo had been looking for a mate for Bamboo, and was under the impression that Massa was a female even after he had arrived (not to put too fine a point on it, in the genitalia department male gorillas are not what you'd expect). The Zoo's Annual Report for 1936 shows Massa in a cage, looking very fetching incidentally, under the caption "Female Mountain Gorilla." In fact, Massa's true sexual identity wasn't revealed until a much anticipated pairing of the two gorillas was attempted. The local press played it up as the wedding of the century. But

The mantle of senior gorilla and soon afterward oldest gorilla in captivity then passed to Massa, Bamboo's one-time fiancee. Massa's story could make a movie—in fact, it did. The movie *Buddy* with Rene Russo is about the relationship of Massa and his onetime owner Gertrude Lintz. In the movie, Mrs. Lintz comes to the Philadelphia Zoo to take a sick baby gorilla back to her home in Brooklyn to nurse it back to health. Actually, she purchased Massa from a sea captain, and raised him in her home along with other chimps and apes, including another baby gorilla she called Buddy, who would achieve greater fame with Ringling Brothers Circus under the name Gargantua. Mrs. Lintz thought Massa was a female and dressed him up in women's clothes. She treated her exotic animals less as pets than children, even putting them to work with household chores. In fact, it was while Massa was scrubbing the kitchen floor, that Mrs. Lintz accidentally

BAMBOO
ANNIVERSARY
AUGUST 5, 1957

Photo by F. Williamson.

Massa was originally thought to be a female. Here he is at the age of five in a photo that appeared in the Zoo's 1936 Annual Report under the caption "Female Mountain Gorilla."

BAMBOO

JOHN ROSOL

SHAMPOO

something happened at the altar. Massa attacked Bamboo, who was almost twice his size at the time. The *Philadelphia Record* on May 26, 1936, reported, "A most embarrassing pre-nuptial discovery was made yesterday at the zoo—the bride is no lady." *The Bulletin* headline read, "Zoo's Gorilla/Wedding is off." *The Record's* story ended with the words, "All wedding gifts will be returned." With that as the starting point of their relationship, is it any wonder that Massa and Bamboo never got along, even though they lived their entire lives side-by-side. Massa was like the pesky kid brother who tormented his older sibling every chance he got.

Massa was never as large as Bamboo, reaching a weight of 350 pounds, compared to the older gorilla's 435. But he had Bamboo's treacherous temperament, keen hand-eye coordination and contempt for the news media. Every year at Massa's birthday party, photographers would line up outside his cage for the birthday boy's photo op. And every year Massa would hurl cake, watermelons, and other treats-turned-debris at them. One year the press photographers conspired before Massa's birthday, and they all showed up wearing yellow slicker rain coats and hats. Like Bamboo, Massa's fame increased with each passing year after he

achieved the status of world's oldest gorilla, which earned him a mention in the *Guinness Book of World Records*. He reigned in his cage at the old Ape and Monkey House for forty-seven years before being moved to the Rare Mammal House in 1983, the same year he had six abscessed teeth removed. His bad teeth had caused him to lose weight over the years and he was down to 175 pounds during his final months. Once magnificent Massa looked like a hobbled old man when he died of a stroke on December 30, 1984, hours after his fifty-fourth birthday party. But he is remembered at the Zoo with a bronze statue of a gorilla in its prime, a statue that has become a symbol of all the great apes that have graced the Zoo with their presence, ornery or otherwise.

Bill Webber of WFIL-Radio raises funds to replace Bamboo, circa 1960.

Visitors enjoy seeing Massa the gorilla.

Massa beats his chest in March 1940.

Massa the Magnificent: This bronze statue of Massa near Primate Reserve became a flower-strewn memorial after the World of Primates fire.

A Lion House Call

Dr. Keith Hinshaw is one of those old-fashioned docs who still makes house calls. It's more a matter of necessity than anything else. After all, his patients can be as big as elephants—literally—or as poisonous as cobras—literally—or dangerous as the beast he has scheduled for surgery this particular Friday morning in October.

Hinshaw is the chief veterinarian at the Philadelphia Zoo, and if ever there was an animal doctor who has been there and done that, it is Hinshaw. His house calls are as literal as his patients' species—Bird House, Reptile House, Rare Animal House.

This morning, for instance, the Zoo vet will make two house calls before trekking to the Carnivora House for the day's most complicated procedure.

Shortly after eight o'clock Dr. Hinshaw sets out from the Zoo's newly opened five-million-dollar Animal Health Center behind the wheel of the official Zoo vet vehicle—a Dodge Ram (a coincidence? I think not!)—and drives down the winding pedestrian paths past trash trucks and other commercial vehicles making deliveries or withdrawals and parks outside the Bird House, an aging structure whose classical facade remains as regal as its interior is faded.

Inside awaits Hinshaw's first patient of the day, a female wrinkled hornbill who is an apparent victim of spousal abuse. At least that's what Bird House keeper Jen Savage suspects happened after she found the female hornbill the other morning sitting listless and disheveled in the pool of water at the bottom of the glass enclosure the lady bird shares with a male.

The female—Savage calls her Sunshine, but most birds in the Zoo don't have names—had refused to eat since. For the last several days, Zoo vets had had to force-feed Sunshine with a rubber hose placed down her gullet into her stomach.

The vet and the keeper walk into the staff-only corridor behind the display cages. Savage retrieves Sunshine with a net, then Hinshaw and his intern, Mason Holland, a Penn vet student, insert a rubber tube down the bird's open beak and squeeze forty milliliters (about one and a third ounces) of brownish formula from a large hypodermic-like device connected to the other end of the tube.

"The main thing is to get it down the esophagus and not the trachea," Hinshaw says. "Otherwise. . . ." The otherwise would be the equivalent of someone force-feeding a liquefied Big Mac and fries into your lungs rather than your stomach.

Breakfast with Sunshine takes a total of fifteen minutes, and soon the vet is on his way to his next house call at the Children's Zoo.

Hinshaw is met at the door of the Children's Zoo animal dorm by Belinda Ogitis who reports that the vet's next patient has taken "a really big poop" the night before. This is great news because the patient, a prehensile-tailed porcupine from South America called a coendou, had undergone an operation the week before to remove a growth from inside its stomach that virtually filled the entire stomach cavity.

"It wasn't a tumor," Hinshaw explains. "It's something called a gastrolith. It weighed 150 grams, about one-third of a pound." Think of a kidney stone the size of your kidney. That's how big the "stomach stone" inside this porcupine's stomach was.

Back at the hospital, the gastrolith sits inside a plastic zip-lock bag. It is greenish brown and cashew shaped, about three-and-a-half inches long and an inch-and-a-half thick.

Hinshaw weighs the Latin porcupine and finds that it has lost weight since the day before. Ogitis suggests that that is probably due to the fact that the little critter had taken its first good dump in more than a year. The vet thinks it was the copious amount of pee rather than poop from the previous night that accounted for the weight loss. Either way the animal looks healthy.

Two down, one to go. Bring on the lady lion.

As you might imagine, there is an exquisite difference between treating an anorexic bird, a constipated porcupine, and a lioness who is about to have her reproductive organs removed. Whereas the first two can make life uncomfortable, miserable even, the latter can, well, eat you.

Keith Hinshaw is a methodical man. Neatly laid out on the floor of the main operating room in the Zoo hospital is the equipment he will use to take down Jezebel, the white lion scheduled to be spayed. There are three medical cases—two black and one blue—a yellow-topped box holding a telinject blowpipe and darts; a brown box containing two pairs of barber shears and lubricating jelly; a cardboard box with extension cords and other electrical equipment; a white tray with clamps, gauze and tape; a green canister of oxygen, a black webbed-nylon litter with aluminum poles; and a green nylon cloth collapsible stretcher on wheels.

This is not a one-human operation. The hospital's other vet and two technicians, two vet school interns, as well as three keepers will be involved in this procedure from beginning until end—six hours later.

It starts with the dart that will bring the lion down. Hinshaw prepares the mixture of tranquilizing drugs that will be used to anesthetize the lion—ketamine, atropine, and xylozine. Fast acting ketamine, says Hinshaw, "is what makes them not bite you." Xylozine keeps them calm and atropine maintains a proper heartbeat while controlling excess saliva.

The drugs—in this case about three milligrams—are put into a plastic hypodermic dart topped with an air-compressed chamber activated upon impact. The needle is nasty looking, thick, and spike-like with two holes about a quarter-inch above the sharp solid point. A rubber sleeve is slipped over the two holes to prevent the fluid from escaping until impact with the animals flesh forces the sleeve back and activates the air injector.

At least that's how it was explained to me.

Over at the Lion House, keeper Steve Cepregi, who joined the Zoo after returning from a tour of duty in Vietnam, looks like he'd rather be back in country than be party to what is about to happen to one of his lions. He is the kind of guy who wears his heart on his sleeve, or in this case his left arm, which bears tattoo likenesses of two of his favorite lions, one of whom, Webster, literally tore the shirt off his back—twice.

"You'd think I would have learned after the first time," Cepregi said of the time Webster lunged at him between the bars when he bent over to pick up a hose outside Webster's cage. The lion caught the neck of Cepregi's shirt with his claws and ripped it from his body.

"Nobody wanted to have anything to do with him," Cepregi said of Webster. "But I'd play with him. Roll his ball to him, stuff like that. Of course the whole time he's trying to kill me."

The same shirt-clawed-off-his-back thing happened the following year. "We became good friends after that," said Cepregi. "Finally he came over to the bars and began rubbing against them and I started stroking him. Before long I could do anything to him. I used to check his teeth."

But always from the other side of the bars. Steve knows how dangerous these animal are. "There are no second chances on this job," he says.

Outside the bars of Jezebel's tiled room Cepregi waits. The white lioness, one of two white lion females at the Zoo, paces as if she knows something's up. Something evil this way comes.

Cepregi coos at Jezebel from deep in his throat, a lion sound that starts with an imperceptible "m" that turns into an "M" followed by a series of delicate "u's" and louder "O's" that end with a soft satisfied "mphh" through the nose. "mmmMMMuuuOOOOOmphh!"

Jezebel answers in kind. She walks over to the bars and leans against them like a cat rubbing your leg under the dinner table. Cepregi scratches her head and back. After a few moments, Jezebel walks over to the far end of her room and lies down. Something is still up and she knows it.

In walks Hinshaw from the main doors to the right of her cage wearing protective eye goggles and carrying a long blowgun with a pistol grip. Ordinarily the sight of the vet is enough to agitate most zoo animals of the higher orders, and Jezebel knows he is clearly up to no good. She lets out a roar that is fierce and scared, somewhere between "I'll kill you" and "Please, don't!"

The vet wastes no time. He steps close to the cage from the opposite end, levels the blowgun on a cross bar, picks his target and fires. Pfffttt! The sound of impact is obscured by the lion's deafening roar-yelp, as brief and sudden as it is loud; like the king of beasts yelling "Yo!"

In that instant Jezebel has yanked the dart from her left hind haunch, leaving the spent cartridge on the tile floor in front of her. Hinshaw is out the door before Cepregi returns to the front of her cage making soothing shushing sounds.

Jezebel licks her sore spot as Cepregi picks up a hose and starts to spray the floor inside her cage until the water catches the plastic dart and flushes it first to the side and finally back down to the trough in front of the cage, where he retrieves it.

After a few minutes the lioness begins pacing frantically back and forth in the back of her cage.

Morning Check Up:
Dr. Keith Hinshaw, Zoo veteri-
narian, weighs a prehensile-
tailed porcupine from the
Children's Zoo following
surgery.

Sleeping Jezebel: *Dr. Donna*
Ialeggio-Pelletier (below left),
assistant veterinarian, assists
Dr. Hinshaw during surgery on
Jezebel the white lion at the
Animal Health Center.

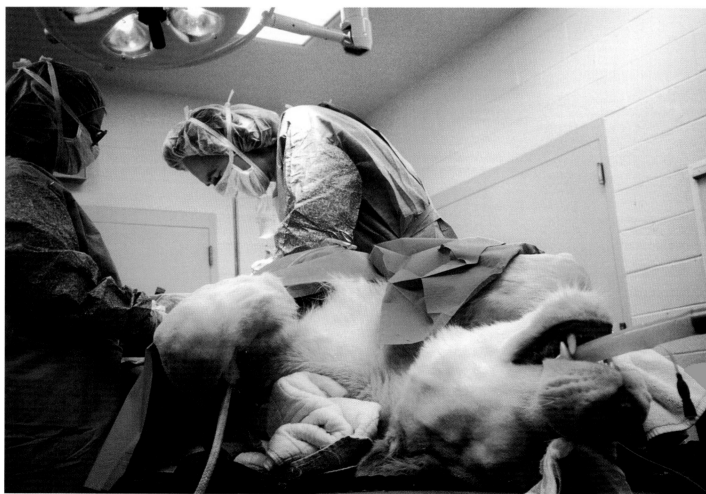

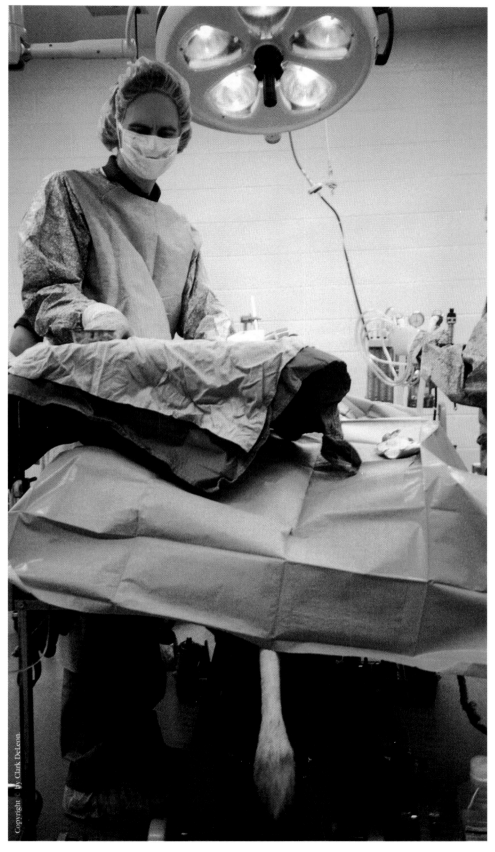

The Telltale Tail:
During surgery at the
Animal Health Center
the procedure looks the
same as it would for a
human patient, except
for one little detail.

Her front paws slip on the slippery floor on one pass, and her rear legs kick out from under her on the way back. Soon it's apparent that it isn't the wet floor that is making her wobbly legged.

As Jezebel careens drunkenly back and forth, her twin sister Vinkel three cages away begins to pace nervously. Outside in the grotto surrounded by a moat, one of the other two lions at the Zoo, either the third female Zenda or Merlin, begins to paw at the aluminum doorway leading to the inner cages. It is as if they sense Jezebel's disorientation.

Ten minutes after being darted, the lioness is stooped over on all fours, her mouth agape, her eyes glassy. Almost imperceptibly she lowers to the floor, her head lolling to one side. She fights the inevitable as long as she can.

After fifteen minutes, Hinshaw returns to the interior of the Lion House. Jezebel stares blankly with unseeing eyes. He reaches between the bars with a pole and touches the lion on her snout and ears. Both twitch at his touch.

The vet and his helpers begin hauling in all the equipment from the hospital, and after twenty-three minutes he tells Cepregi that he is ready to enter the lion's den. The door is unlocked and Hinshaw walks inside. "Theoretically, it's safe," he says, theoretically joking. He is slightly built, and looks even smaller standing next to the motionless white beast at his feet.

He gives Jezebel another injection of ketamine, which wears off as quickly as it takes effect, and then summons his crew to enter the cage with the various boxes from the hospital. While Hinshaw shaves a strip of fur off Jezebel's right rear leg to find a vein for the IV, fellow Zoo vet Donna Ialeggio-Pelletier examines Jezebel's eyes and teeth, putting salve on her open eyes, and checking her gums for possible signs of inadequate blood flow in response to the anesthesia. As she leans forward, the lioness exhales into Dr. Ialeggio-Pelletier's face, and the vet waves her hand up and down in front of her own face in the international signal meaning, "Oy! Such breath!"

At one point a total of five people are ministering to the prostrate lioness, not counting the two extra keepers Mike Seeley from the Elephant House and Bob Pittman from Carnivore Kingdom, who have shown up to assist in carrying Jezebel out of her cage and in to the van for the trip back to the hospital.

Six people carry the litter carrying Jezebel. The move goes smoothly, and a class full of schoolchildren arriving at the Lion House never even notice the lion on the stretcher being loaded on the truck backed up to the Lion House doors.

Back at the hospital the lioness is transferred onto a hydraulic operating table and weighed. This adaptable table can accommodate all but the largest animals—it was designed for horses. First things first, Hinshaw must find a way of securing his patient to the table—just in case. He returns from a back room holding restraining ropes of various sizes. He chooses a large rope and ties off one of the lions back legs attaching the other end to a metal cleat underneath the table. "Should we pull the legs back like this," the Zoo vet asks. "I don't think these leads will stretch that far," says Susan Isackson, the vet technician, gesturing to the wires attached to the lion and leading to an electrical monitor. "I'm not worried about that, I'm worried about the surgical approach," says Hinshaw, tying off the other leg about mid-calf, and securing it under the table. The ropes are looped around twice to prevent too much pressure on one part of the leg. Her front legs are tied across the front of her chest, each leg secured by a separate rope tied off under the table.

The scale says the says Jezebel weighs a not-so-svelte 288 pounds. Her excess weight becomes a problem for the two surgeons once the neutering operation commences. Her stomach is surrounded by so much fat, that the vets have a hard time finding the two horns of her uterus containing her ovaries. "She's nutritionally successful," teases veterinary technician Sandy Skeb-McCampbell, "but she's not a good mom. When Jezzy has babies we have to take care of them." Skeba-McCampbell is the first one to refer to the lion by its name.

Jezebel has given birth to two litters, rejecting her offspring both times. Because of this, Jezebel's lion cubs had to be raised by hand by humans. That, and the fact that her genetic stock is "well represented" in the worldwide zoo lion population, were factors in the decision to have her neutered. She has a contraceptive implant about the size of a triple-A battery, which was quickly removed from the top of her shoulder following a one-inch incision before the major surgery began. Why not simply leave the contraceptive device in rather than risk this surgery?

"Since implants are hormonal there is a greater risk of pathological changes in her breasts and uterus, up to and including cancer," explains Dr. Ialeggio-Pelletier.

Before the surgery, Skeba-McCampbell shaves the snow-white fur off Jezebel's abdomen, exposing four nipples and skin as pink as bubble gum. The fur is vacuumed into a plastic bag and sealed. This will be turned over to Karl Kranz, senior vice president for animal affairs, for his inspection.

Once the lioness is rolled into the sterile operating room, all the humans in attendance are required to don hospital gowns, masks, and foot coverings. Skeba-McCampbell begins washing Jezebel's stomach with disinfectant soap, while commenting to Seeley, the elephant keeper who has stayed to watch the operation, that spaying a lion that has had cubs in not like a spaying a house cat, where a pet vet might be able to complete fifteen such procedures in a day.

Dr. Ialeggio-Pelletier returns from a telephone call with some news about a patient. "He's blocked," she announces, regarding a monkey that can't urinate. "Well, he's going to have to wait until we're done here," sighs Dr. Hinshaw.

The two Zoo vets adjourn to an adjoining washroom where they scrub for surgery, donning sterile smocks. They emerge from the room and after being assisted into sterile latex gloves, they stand over the lion with their hands held palms inward near their chests, fingers pointing to the ceiling like priests about to offer mass, as they wait for the trays containing sterilized surgical instruments to be opened by Skeba-McCampbell and Isackson. Dr. Hinshaw opens the final cloth sealed with a strip of adhesive paper and arranged his tools. Jezebel lets out a deep anesthetized breath, just as Hinshaw and Ialeggio-Pelletier begin to secure the sterilized paper surgical covering over the lion's belly. In the end only a rectangular section of skin, eight inches by four inches is exposed. Hinshaw uses surgical scissors to make the rectangle a few inches longer. Then he takes up his scalpel and starts the operation with an eight-inch incision down the middle of Jezebel's abdomen.

The surgery goes slowly. Jezebel has a good four-to-six inch layer of fat between her epidermis and her internal organ cavity, plus more inter-abdominal fat. That poses problems finding her uterus, which is found behind her full bladder. First the bladder must be emptied. Hinshaw tells his vet student, Holland, who is taking Jezebel's anal temperature, that he is about to squeeze the bladder. "Tell me if you see anything come out," he says. To which Holland replies, "I'm in a pretty vulnerable position here." Nothing comes out, so the bladder has to be emptied by catheter syringe. Three and a half syringes holding two ounces of urine each are removed. The bladder is smaller but with all the fat, there's still not much room to work. "I should have put her on a crash diet," Hinshaw says.

During the surgery, Holland and Skeba-McCampbell are continually recording the lion's vital signs—heartbeat, respiration. Holland reports that Jezebel's heart rate is about fifty beats per minute. What should a lion's pulse rate be?, I ask. "Seventyish, almost like a human's," says Holland. Adds Skeba-McCampbell, "It's hard to tell because we don't get the chance to take a lion's pulse unless it's anesthetized."

Drs. Hinshaw and Ialeggio-Pelletier labor over the anesthetized lion for five hours nonstop. During that time various keepers from the Zoo donned scrubs and masks and entered the operating room to observed the surgery. "Ooooo, my back," says Hinshaw rolling his shoulders. Ialeggio-Pelletier's long braided ponytail coils around inside the back of her surgical hairnet like a sleeping black snake with a blue ring.

Finally, both horns of Jezebel's uterus (unlike humans, but like cows and horses, lions have two sets of ovaries and can conceive in each) are located and removed. The tube is reddish pink, while the ovaries are a deeper purplish red that resemble a flattened chicken liver in size and shape. It takes about an hour to close up the lion's abdomen and it's a little before four o'clock when Jezebel is wheeled out of the operating room, loaded on to the van and returned to her cage in the Carnivora House. Hinshaw has timed the anesthesia to within ten minutes of the big cat waking up. And he doesn't want to be the first face Jezebel sees when she opens her eyes.

The big cat wakes up, looks down at her shaved belly and begins licking her stitches.

Meanwhile the vets have another house call to make. There's this monkey, you see, and he can't pee.

Two of the Missed: Before the fi[re], Octavian the young white gibbon and Jingga the baby orangutan became playmates. They are seen here in 1995 in the World of Primates. In the wild these species would never interact.

Gorilla My Dreams: Kola the baby gorilla loved her brother Chaka and sought him out in the World of Primates outdoor play area before Chaka moved to the Cincinnati Zoo in 1993.

Copyright © by Ron Austin.

Copyright © by Ann Hartman

One of the Living: *Golden lion-headed tamarins like this one (above) survived the World of Primates fire because they were sleeping in the Discovery House adjacent to the main building.*

Top Left:
Child is Father to the Ape: *In Cincinnati Chaka matured into the very picture of his handsome father John. Chaka will be the dominant male of the new gorilla family at Primate Reserve.*

Copyright © by Ann Mai Byrnes.

Like Father, Like Son: *In the months before he left Philadelphia in 1993, Chaka tags along after his father John in the World of Primates.*

The Saddest Christmas Story

Whenever I think about the fire in the World of Primates that killed twenty-three of the Zoo's most popular and beloved animals early morning hours on Christmas Eve 1995, I think about a passage I read years ago in a book I was leafing through. I can neither remember the name of the book or its author, but I recall the ache I felt when I read the following words, words that still seem to hang in the air like smoke on a bright black winter night.

"It was very sad. It was so sad that it is impossible even now to say how sad it really was. Well, that's the way it is. If you don't have children, you couldn't possibly understand."

It was so sad that it is impossible even now for many people at the Zoo to say how sad it really was. I see it in the pain in their eyes, in the grief beyond tears or explanation. I hear it in their voices, in the way that some of them hurry through the telling, and in the way that others can't stop talking about it, as if by continuing to tell they can somehow change the ending of that saddest of Christmas stories. The ending that came upon a midnight clear, when a smoldering fire in the ceiling of the cinderblock holding/exhibit building was discovered and the Fire Department alerted at 12:44 a.m.

Some Zoo people were surrounded by loved ones and visiting relatives sleeping in spare beds during the holiday when they were awakened by a telephone call in the middle of the night. Others heard the news on the car radio on the way to work the next morning. Others arrived at work and wondered why there were so many TV news vans around the Zoo so early on a day when the Zoo was closed to the public. Others heard the news on TV as the family sat down to Sunday breakfast, their children bursting into tears over their cornflakes. Others were on vacation elsewhere when CNN or a grief-stricken relative calling on the phone interrupted their holiday with the terrible news. And others were there before the firemen had rolled up their hoses.

Electrician Hank Caratura rushed to the Zoo from home in Manayunk after a frantic phone call. He had the keys to a locked steel door in a room controlling the electrical power supply that had to be shut off before firefighters could safely enter the fire-damaged water-soaked buildings.

When Karl Kranz, senior vice president of animal affairs, arrived at the scene, Andy Baker, curator of small mammals and primates, was already there. Both men had been called at home by John Ffinch, the curator of birds, whose phone number happened to be the first one dialed by the Security Office. Ffinch had no details to give Kranz over the phone, other than there was a fire at the World of Primates. Kranz hung up, then called the Zoo back a minute later. "Was there smoke inside the building?," he asked. "Yes," he was told. He rushed to the scene, his heart sinking at the sight of so many fire trucks and hose lines. Then he saw Baker who told him the news. It was as bad as it could get. Except for the marmosets and tamarins housed in the adjoining Discovery House, all the primates were gone. Together they entered the building to bring out the dead.

Ken Rebechi was one of the first Zoo maintenance staffers to enter the gorilla compound and begin removing bodies. They looked so peaceful, he said. If it wasn't for the soot and ash covering their bodies, he would have thought they were sleeping rather than dead. And when they carried the gorillas, orangutans, gibbons, and lemurs away, left behind was a perfect outline of the contours of their bodies on the clean floor, right down to the subtle layered fringe of fur on the outer edges, a soot-free silhouette that gave no evidence of struggle. They died in their sleep, all of them, snuggled together in their sleeping chambers.

Only John, only magnificent John, the father-leader of the clan of six lowland gorillas, was found somewhere else. His body was discovered in a caged tunnel, like a hallway between the gorilla family room and the outdoor enclosure. Had John sensed that something was wrong? Had he awakened to investigate a strange noise, or perhaps, an odor? Whatever John's intentions, slumber overtook him. He was found in a sleeping position on his back in the tunnel cage, so peaceful and lifelike that Ken Rebechi wondered if perhaps he wasn't sleeping. And when he had to climb over the gorilla's massive and still-warm body in the cramped tunnel to assist in removing John's body, Ribechi placed his knee on John's chest, the great ape let out a sudden audible breath. PAHHaahhhhh!

It was John's last gasp. And for a terrifying moment or two, Rebechi thought it was his last gasp as well.

One by one the twenty-three corpses—some as large and bulky as refrigerators, others as small and soft as teddy bears—were carried from their sleeping quarters in the World of Primates to the stainless steel walk-in cooler in the necropsy lab of the Penrose Building. Besides the six gorillas, there were three Bornean orangutans, four white-handed gibbons, six ring-tailed lemurs, two ruffed-lemurs, and two mongoose lemurs. They were waiting for Dr. Virginia Pierce, the Zoo pathologist, when she arrived at 7:00 a.m. Christmas Eve to begin the necropsies. Waiting for her on the examination table was John.

Only five zoos in the United States employ full-time pathologists—the Bronx, the National, San Diego, and St. Louis are the others—something Philadelphia has done since 1874. It was the Philadelphia Zoo's pioneering work in animal autopsies (necropsies) by Dr. Henry Chapman that established the standard by which other zoos would be measured. Every animal that dies at the Zoo undergoes a necropsy to determine the cause of death and the condition of the animal at the time of death. In 1876, Chapman described what happens to the animals following the necropsy: "In every case where the animals were of sufficient value, they have been properly prepared and placed in museums in the Academy of Natural Sciences, or of the University of Pennsylvania. . . . The animals being either stuffed, their skeletons mounted or their internal organs preserved."

More than one hundred years later, the necropsy protocols had not changed, except by degree and sophistication. Animals of "sufficient value"—and these rare and endangered animals were of enormous scientific value—underwent a battery of measurements, blood tests, taking of tissue samples, and removal of internal organs to be shipped to the Species Survival Plan (SSP) coordinator and other governmental and private scientific agencies. The U.S. Fish and Wildlife Service Forensic Laboratory in Ashland, Oregon, for instance, requested tissue samples and bones from one male and one female of each species that died in the fire. The facility is a library of known animal specimens, and the tissue samples and blood work on the lemurs was immediately useful in the prosecution of an animal dealer illegally trafficking in endangered species. The identity of individual species of certain animals are difficult to determine, and when the genetic information of the animals in question matched that of the dead lemurs, it helped prove the government's case. Any soft tissue remains of the twenty-three dead primates that were not preserved for scientific purposes were cremated. Their ashes were preserved for eventual burial on the site of the Primate Reserve.

The necropsy on John alone would take Dr. Pierce five hours to complete. "He was huge," she said. "And the phone kept ringing with more requests for tissue and other samples." Before she began the necropsy, however, Dr. Pierce waited for some of the keepers like Ann Hess and Julie Unger-Smith to say their goodbyes.

Perhaps, there is no one at the Zoo whose personal grief over the deaths of those animals is more evident than Julie Unger-Smith, lead keeper at the World of Primates. You can almost see the hole in her heart. Months afterward, some people would break into tears for her loss when they spoke to her about the fire.

She had been spending the night at her fiancee's family's house when the call came. "I was pulled out of bed and brought to the phone," she says. It was Andy Baker. "I heard later that Andy was absolutely tormented about how to tell the keepers," she recalls. "He's always been a very straightforward person and there was no easy way to say it. He just said, 'Julie, something bad has happened. . . .'"

Tears overtake her story. She recovers and continues. "'Which one? Which animal?,' I said to Baker. I knew he couldn't be calling to say that one of the moats was overflowing or a rail broke.

Names Not Forgotten:
This memorial to the animals in the World of Primates fire has the names of all twenty-three that perished.

Grieving the Loss:
Thousands of schoolchildren contributed artwork and poetry to the Memorial Gallery established after the fire.

Madonna of the Forest: Two of the most beloved animals in the World of Primates were Rita the inquisitive orangutan and Jingga, her even more inquisitive daughter.

I knew someone had died. I absolutely knew. And I knew it was an animal. Looking back, if it had been one of my co-workers, it would have been devastating. But I knew it was an animal. But which one. Oh, God, which one?

"I just couldn't comprehend what he said. He said, 'There was a fire and . . . all the animals died at the World of Primates.' And, it's so goofy now, but I remember saying, 'All the gorillas?' And he said, 'yes.' And I went through all the species. 'All the orangs?' And he said yes. 'All the gibbons?'

And he said, 'yes.' 'All the lemurs. . . .'

"It just seems like a dream. It does not seem real. You know, as a keeper you're always looking at your animals and you're always thinking that your life span is probably going to be longer than theirs. And you say so many goodbyes in the zoo field. Either animals are dying or part of the success of zoos is to see animals shipped off to other zoos to be mated. But it's always difficult to say goodbye. Sometimes, just to get by, you have to pretend they are in another zoo someplace."

John's Family: One of John's two mates in the World of Primates was Snickers, already stooped with arthritis, but still able to care for her baby Maandazi.

Julie got to say goodbye to John and the others in the necropsy room. "I got to hold John's hand," she says through tears. "It's just so ironic. In this job you get so close to them. But this was the closest I ever was to them. It was so sad. I wonder sometimes how we all got through it."

Dr. Pierce, who was seven months pregnant with her third child at the time of the fire, discovered during the necropsies that Samantha, John's mate, was pregnant. She was too busy at the time to allow herself an emotional reaction. "I believe that we humans are obligated to get every bit of information we can from every encounter with wild animals," she says. There was so much to do. In fact, it didn't hit her until months later. "I didn't cry until March," she says. "I didn't cry until my son, Dawson, figured out what happened. He had a stuffed toy gibbon named Small Face. We were in the living room in the middle of the afternoon when he realized that they were really dead. And what that meant. We both just cried and cried."

Most of the men I spoke to in the Animal Department, keepers and curators, said they didn't cry. Not publicly, anyway. "I have a hard time with public displays of emotion," said Andy Baker, whose deep pain shows through dry eyes. The closest Baker came to breaking down, he says, was much later when he saw a photo of Jingga the baby orangutan holding the hand of Octavian the young gibbon (see page 88), two species that would never be in such cordial contact in the wild. "I have a hard time looking at that picture," he says.

Hoofstock keeper Ken Pelletier said the same thing about Jingga being the reason he came closest to losing it in front of people. "That's not something I do," he said of public tears. Pelletier had arrived for work that morning to discover the tragedy overnight. He volunteered to assist with the necropsy process, helping to record information as the pathologist dictated. He helped with one of the gibbons, "And then they brought in the baby orang, Jingga, who was three or four years old at the time," he says. "Since I was open relief I spent a lot of time down [at the World of Primates] the first summer I was here. I got to know Jingga pretty well. And when they brought

her in, I said, 'I'm sorry. I can't help any more.' And I went home."

Jingga and her mother, Rita, (see page 93) were particular favorites for many Zoo staffers. "At lunchtime you would go out and visit your favorite animal," says Mary Heider, the Zoo's annual giving coordinator. "And Rita was mine. She was so human, so close to us. She'd recognize members of the staff. She'd come up to the glass to see me. She always wanted to see what you had in your bag. Her eyes were worth a million dollars." Ann Marie Byrnes, Zoo docent and photographer, was fond of Rita and Jingga as well. "We'd [she and her husband Tom Hartman, both of whose photos appear in this book] be there taking photographs and Rita would come up to the window and I'd show her pictures we'd taken," Byrnes says. "She look intently at the photo and when she was done she'd look up into my eyes as if to say, 'Next!' and then she'd look down and wait for me to show her a new picture."

Perhaps the most noticeable difference at the Zoo since the fire, other than the physical absence of the actual apes, has been the sounds of silence. "It hit me the other day, the absence of the gibbons," says Julie Unger-Smith. "To hear that again, the cry of the gibbons. It's like a song through the whole Zoo. It's like a hooting, this series of ups and down. These trills they would do. Just beautiful long calls."

The legacy of the fire has been far reaching. It has touched zoos all around the world. It was the "But the grace of God . . ." event that every zoo person fears—to have so many animals die while in the zoo's care. "It's almost unspeakable," says Julie. "Pete Hoskins actually said to us later, 'We let the animals down.' Not that we were taking blame for doing any one thing wrong, but that they were in our care when this happened. Pete genuinely felt the pain, for himself and for us."

Not surprisingly, the daily focus of the Zoo changed dramatically in the aftermath of the fire. Things that were once taken for granted no longer were taken for granted, especially issues of animal safety. And the Zoo's larger identity has been indelibly scorched by the midnight flames of that Christmas Eve.

Z is for Zebra: *Reflected in his own thirst, this zebra takes a sip of water from the moat in Phase One of the African Plains Exhibit.*

Simple as ABC

In zoo people parlance, popular animals that visitors want to see are known as ABC animals.

Here's what you need to know about ABC animals. When you get to the end, Z is for zebra and you're done. Not only is Z the last letter in the alphabet, but zebra is the only animal that begins with that letter. Unless you count the zebu, and I don't know why anyone would.

Other one-word wonder animal letters are Q is for quail, Y is for is for yak and, believe it or not, U is for uakari, which is a type of monkey found in western Brazil and eastern Peru. But for all intents and purposes, when it comes to ABC animals the letter U may as well go the way of the letter X because there is no animal name that begins with an X, with the possible exception of a dyslexic foX.

ABC animals are supposed to be familiar and alphabet friendly. A is for alligator, antelope, ape, or anteater. In a stretch A can be for aardvark, but never for aoudad, anole, or anhinga.

B can be for bear, bat, beaver, bison, or buffalo. Even boa. But B can never be for banteng, binturong, blesbok, or budgerigar.

C, of course, can be for cat, camel, cobra, chimpanzee, and coyote. Chameleon is a coin toss. But don't ever try C for cacomistle, capybara, coscoroba, or coypu.

D is for dik-dik, and I don't care who knows it.

E is pretty much up to you. Eagle, elephant, elk, eland, emu—everything but echidna.

F is for frog, as well it should be.

As for G, this much we know. Gnever, gnever, gnever, can G be for gnu.

American bison.

Photo by F. Williamson.

Above:
American elk.

Left:
Bactrian camel.

Guas and Guarina, the Zoo's first orangutans, arrived in 1931 and both set records for longevity.

A GREAT, DEPRESSING ZOOSTORY

Considering what was about to happen in the years to come, 1930 was a very good year for Philadelphia. At Shibe Park in North Philadelphia, Connie Mack's Athletics had won their second consecutive World Series championship with a talent-studded lineup that is still ranked among the best major league teams ever. A few blocks away at Baker Bowl the perennially woeful but always hopeful Phillies had acquired a slugger named Chuck Klein who smashed 40 homers, 59 doubles, and scored 158 runs while batting in another 170 runs and hitting for an average of .386, setting a National League batting record that stands to this day. In Center City office building construction was booming and ground had been broken for no fewer than a dozen skyscrapers, including the architectural wonder at Twelfth and Market Streets that would be headquarters to PSFS, the Philadelphia Savings Fund Society.

In 1930 more Philadelphians owned their own homes than residents of any other city thanks in great part to the astounding number—3,400—of building and loan associations thriving in every neighborhood. Philadelphia ranked third among America's largest cities with a population of 1,950,961, an increase of 7 percent since 1920, and it was surrounded by affluent suburban communities growing even faster.

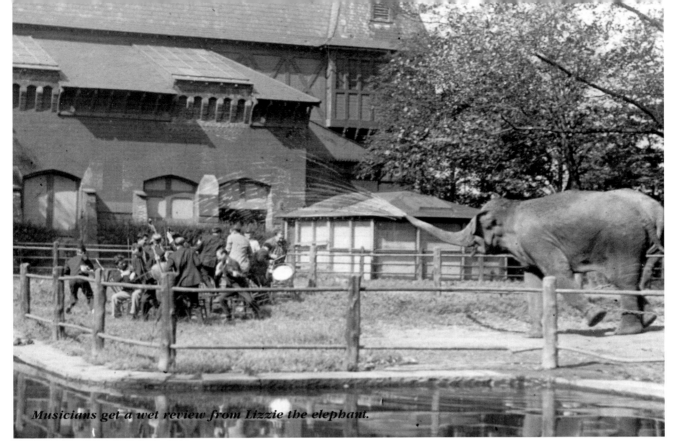

Musicians get a wet review from Lizzie the elephant.

Times were good at the Zoo. Plans were underway for major renovations in the southern end of the garden to be funded by the Pennsylvania Railroad in exchange for several acres of ground. The Zoo, which had started at thirty-three acres and grown to fifty, was now the size it is today—forty-two acres. In the autumn of 1930, Parkway designer Paul Cret, winner of that year's Philadelphia Award, was named official architect of the Zoological Society and work was begun on Cret's design for a new South Entrance to the Zoo including Gate House and parking areas. All in all, the less-than-prophetic headline on the *Inquirer*'s business page on January 3, 1930, seemed to be accurate: "Philadelphia Faces New Year Confident of Brighter Future."

But the bright future would have to endure startling darkness. American business had taken a bullet during the stock market crash of 1929, but Philadelphia, because of the diversity of its manufacturing-based economy, didn't start to stagger until the end of 1930. That's when the first of the fifty banks that would fail in the city by 1933 folded. Even worse, by 1934 almost half—more than sixteen hundred—of the city's building and loan associations had shut their doors, sparking a stampede of residential mortgage foreclosures. On one block of North Van Pelt Street

alone, twenty-three out of sixty homes were repossessed between 1932 and 1934. The city's real estate tax base collapsed. Philadelphia Mayor J. Hampton Moore responded to the crisis by firing thirty-five hundred city employees. Police and firefighters were forced to take two-week vacations without pay. During one six-month period, twelve thousand men passed through a homeless shelter operated out of an eight-story loft belonging to the Baldwin Locomotive Works. Local hospitals began reporting, not just malnutrition, but "definite cases of starvation." After the lights were turned on atop the proud new skyscraper that began dominating the Center City's nighttime skyline when it opened in 1932, the running joke during the Great Depression was that the huge red letters PSFS stood for "Philadelphians Slowly Facing Starvation."

And if people were starving, what about the animals? "The daily menu for these animals," reported the December–January 1931 *Bulletin of the Philadelphia Zoological Society* about the Zoo's two nineteen-year-old hippopotamuses, "consists of 12 quarts white potatoes, 10 quarts rolled oats, 10 quarts bran, 4 heads cabbage and about 52 lbs. of mixed hay. The cost of each daily is approximately $2.65, the largest cost of feeding any animal in the zoo, includ-

Many zookeepers started as pony boys.

Ticket Booth for the Baby Pet Zoo which was the first children's zoo in the country.

ing the elephant." This at a time when women working in Philadelphia garment factories were being paid less than $6.58 per week.

If it took the city a full year to begin to recognize and suffer the harsher realities of such desperate times, it took the Zoo even longer. "Due supposedly to the business depression membership applications have not been coming in as well as usual," reported the same issue of the Zoo *Bulletin* regarding the paltry total of eight new dues-paying members signed up December 1930 and January 1931. During the same period the year before, the Zoo had attracted seventy-six new members, that total representing a decline from the ninety-seven who had applied for membership in December and January the year before that. In April 1931, the Zoo responded to the dramatic decline in revenue from membership by increasing the price of admission from thirty-five to fifty cents for adults and from for fifteen to twenty-five cents for children.

As might be expected, this did nothing to improve attendance, which dropped from 352,000 in 1930 to 244,000 in 1931 to 152,000 in 1932—a decrease of 200,000. At the same time the city of Philadelphia, with its frugal mayor and City Council, reduced the city appropriation to the Zoo from $50,000 to $37,500 in 1931 to $25,000 in 1932. Predictably, the Zoo suffered the worst financial crisis of its history. The sixtieth Annual Report of the Zoological Society read to members and loan holders at the annual meeting on April 28, 1932, opened with an unprecedented "An Appeal for the Zoo" rather than the traditional "Report of the Board of Directors." Citing a one-year deficit of $37,375 for the fiscal year ending February 29, 1932, Society President Williams B. Cadwalader railed at the city's reduced appropriation, comparing the generous municipal governmental support of the city zoos in Chicago, Washington, New York, Detroit, and St. Louis (ranging from a high of $662,000 in Chicago to $250,000 in St. Louis) to $25,000 in Philadelphia, "an amount utterly inadequate for its maintenance."

The Zoo's appeals took on an increasingly desperate tone during the darkest days of the Depression. "It is a deplorable fact that the financial condition of the Zoological Garden is alarming," reported the August–September 1932 Zoo *Bulletin* in a sentence where the words *deplorable* and *alarming* could easily have been reversed without changing its meaning. "This, one of the largest and finest zoos in the world, is nearing a point where it will be obliged to close its gates unless adequate funds are soon available. There is no half way. If a collection of 3,300 animals is to be kept there must be sufficient food and an adequate number of men to feed and manage them successfully."

In 1932—a leap year—the Zoo's operating deficit leaped to $45,386. Gate receipts were down by a total

Above: Elephant ride. Right: Camel ride.

of $42,612 over the previous dismal year. In his appeal, Cadwalader wrote, "Every possible effort has been made to effect economies. . . . Salaries have been reduced to a minimum. . . . No new animals have been acquired except those that have been donated. . . ." Indeed, over the next several years the number of specimens in the zoo's collection dropped by more than 1,000—from 3,419 to 2,784 to 2,530 to 2,449 to 2,350—birds and reptiles accounting for the largest decline.

The 1933 Report of the Board of Directors, written by Board Secretary Radcliffe Cheston, Jr., took on a poetic, almost evangelistic tone:

A park is like a lightning rod, drawing discontent into the ground. It is a place where those burdened

with troubles and grievances, either real or imagined, can find some measure of relief from the hard reality of city streets and so lose themselves amid interesting and beautiful surroundings rather than to give way under stress of their troubles and find an outlet through sordid means and even unlawful acts. Disaster, discontent, grief, violence are things not avoided, but averted. A park is regenerative. A Zoo within a park is that, and more than that—to a child an earthly Paradise. . . .

At all times, especially in a time of great stress, such as this, a garden or park is of inestimable value to a large city. For this reason, if for no other, those having authority over the affairs of the city should more jealously guard your Garden and see that it be kept intact and open to the citizens of today and the future.

Philadelphia's five daily newspapers (*The Inquirer, The Bulletin*, the two *Public Ledgers*, morning and evening, and the *Record*) rallied behind the zoo, but none more forcefully than publisher J. David Stern's *Philadelphia Record*. All the papers lavished valuable feature space on the coming and goings of animals and other developments at the Zoo, but there was an edge to the *Record*'s reportage and editorials about the plight of the Zoo.

"It's the same old story," began a *Record* story on the 1933 Annual Report announcing the Zoo's $45,386 deficit, "everyone thinks the [Zoo's] performance is swell, but hardly anybody ever attends. . . . Dr. Williams Cadwalader, president of the society, warned that the animals will have the be shot or gassed unless the old institution receives adequate support."

As might be expected from a city with a well-earned reputation for possessing a generous and charitable nature, the citizens of Philadelphia responded to the Zoo's plight. First through spontaneous and much-publicized donations from

Artist's conception of Goat Hill at the planned "Free Modern Zoo" of the future. Center City rises in the background.

Philadelphia area schoolchildren, as well as from longtime and newly enlisted members of the Zoological Society.

With the election of Franklin Roosevelt and the coming of the New Deal, the Zoo received much needed relief from a number of federal "alphabet soup" agencies created to put unemployed men to work. Over the next few years under banners of the CWA (Civil Works Administration), the WPA (Works Progress Administration), and the LWD (Local Works Division), hundreds of skilled and unskilled laborers and white-collar workers were employed. Sewer pipes were laid, retaining walls built, concrete walkways repaved, and the grounds landscaped. A. E. Wohlert, owner of the Garden Nurseries in Narberth, donated fifteen hundred Japanese cherry, flowering crab apple, spruce, and other trees to the Zoo and he offered to personally oversee the planting. By autumn of 1934 the Zoo *Bulletin* was almost boasting of the "vast improvements in cleanliness and sanitation" that had been accomplished "during the so-called depression." Said the *Bulletin*, "To one who has not visited

the Garden for several years awaits a surprise in the very marked improvement that have recently been made . . . changing a dreary, rather barren landscape into a beautiful flowering garden with spacious enclosures for birds and animals."

Despite flagging attendance, public interest in the Zoo was demonstrated in a dramatic way on July 15, 1933, when the Zoo opened its gates to any and all with no admission price. By the end of the Zoo's first ever Free Day almost 70,000 people had passed through the gates. "These astounding figures should forever set to rest the minds of those who ever thought that the Zoo had lost its popularity and was not one of Philadelphia's greatest assets," crowed the Zoo *Bulletin*. (Three years later the Zoo would again open its gates for nine days of free admissions to generate support for a publicly funded "Free and Modern Zoo." Those nine days attracted more visitors than the total for most previous *years*. From Saturday October 3 to Sunday October 11, 1936, a total of 352,000 men, women, and children passed through the gates—a record 154,000 on the final Sunday.)

One casualty of the Zoo's ongoing financial difficulties was Garden Director C. Emerson Brown, who resigned in 1935 after seventeen years in that post. His replacement was a personable Scottish-born professor from Harvard, Dr. Roderick Macdonald, a publicity conscious administrator who wooed the media and made scores of public speaking appearances on

Large crowds took advantage of Free Week in 1936.

behalf of the Zoo. Macdonald instituted a more scientific tone to the Zoo *Bulletin* and the Zoo administration. Macdonald hired the Zoo's first full-time curators, a primatologist named Michael Tomilin, and a young herpetologist from the Toldedo Zoo named Roger Conant, a man destined to be one of the Zoo's most flamboyant characters and successful advocates during his thirty-six-year career. "When I arrived at the zoo in 1935, the old buildings were virtually held together with the proverbial paint and bailing wire," Conant wrote in his autobiography, *A Field Guide to the Life and Times of Roger Conant.* "It would take many of us, working together for years, to restore the zoo to its proper position as a leading institution."

Despite the hard times, the 1930s was a turnaround decade for the Zoo. The last front page "An Appeal for the Zoo" during the Depression appeared in the 1936 Annual Report. In it, president Williams Cadwalader wrote, "I am happy to report that the affairs of the Zoological Society and the condition of the Zoological Garden are greatly improved." Over at the Laboratory of Comparative Pathology, renamed the Penrose Research Laboratory in 1935 in honor of former Society President Dr. Charles B. Penrose, breakthrough research in animal nutrition and disease prevention continued to enhance the Zoo's international reputation in the scientific community. Dr. Herbert L Ratcliffe, building on twenty years of nutritional research by Dr. E. P. Corson-White, developed a recipe for a vitamin-packed meal called "monkey cake" (later "zoo cake") that would revolutionize the diet of captive primates. Although the brownish blocks of meat, wheat meal, soybean meal, cornmeal, rolled oats, peanut meal, alfalfa-leaf meal, oyster-shell flour, salt, and cod liver oil *looked* unattractive (one letter writer in the newspaper described monkey cake as looking like "mouldy scrapple") the results spoke for themselves. The annual death rate among primates was more than cut in half—from 25 percent to 12 percent—in the five years after monkey cake became the daily diet for a variety of zoo animals, including prairie dogs, squirrels, porcupines, agoutis, raccoons, coatis, and kinkajous. "But our echidna is in good health after 36 years on a daily ration of one pint of milk and one raw egg," Ratcliffe wrote in 1940.

In the garden the unprecedented health and longevity of the Zoo's primates, especially Bamboo, the longest-lived gorilla in captivity, continued to attract attention from the public and scientists alike. The arrival in 1936 of Massa, the gorilla destined to be Bamboo's heir apparent in longevity, was another step in cementing the Zoo's reputation for success in rearing large primates. Also that year, the Zoo took the first steps toward establishing what would become the Children's Zoo with the construction of the Model Dairy Barn funded by the Philadelphia Interstate Dairy Council (at the time an estimated 17 percent of Philadelphia schoolchildren had never seen a live cow).

Dr. Macdonald launched a weekly radio program on KYW on February 15, 1936, called "Let's Visit the Zoo." After ten weeks it became Roger Conant's weekly vehicle to inform the public for the next thirty-three years. Dr. Macdonald's tenure as managing director of the Society was the shortest of any superintendent or director in the garden's history. After a little more than a year in the job, he was replaced by frugal business manager Freeman H. Shelly, whose decades of service to the Zoo are commemorated by the Shelly Building, the current administration building named in his honor. Under Shelly's prudent fiscal policies the Zoo would emerge from the final days of the Great Depression and face the new challenge of operating a public zoo in the midst of the gathering storm of the greatest war in human history.

But first, Monkey Island.

Guest Star:
Leo from Hollywood

For more than fifty years the movies made by Metro-Goldwyn-Mayer Studios have been identified with the studio's trademark—a roaring lion. The original MGM logo lion was a young African lion captured in the Nubian Desert. And Leo was his name-o. Leo was already famous when the MGM lion arrived at the Philadelphia Zoo on October 25, 1933, for what was supposed to be a winter respite from life on the road as a traveling star. "Lucky Leo" he was dubbed in the press because over the years since his arrival in America, Leo had survived two train wrecks, a flood on the Mississippi River, a California earthquake, and a studio explosion. Instead of remaining a few months, Leo lived out the rest of his life in Philadelphia as the Lion House's leading guest star. He was found dead in his cage of an apparent heart attack by John McMullen, head lion keeper, on the morning of February 26, 1935. Lucky Leo had lived to be twenty.

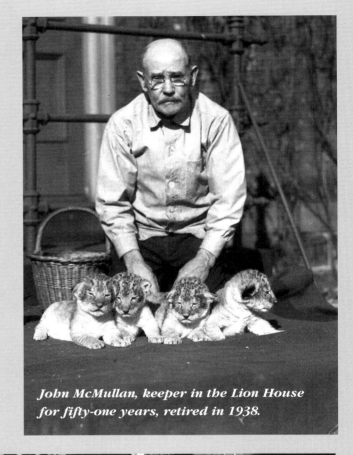

John McMullan, keeper in the Lion House for fifty-one years, retired in 1938.

Photo by Kauffeld

Leo, the MGM lion.

Photo by Kauffeld

Star Boarder: Goliath

Never did a short-timer at the Philadelphia Zoo get as much publicity as Goliath, the three-ton sea elephant, who arrived the same month as Lucky Leo—October 1933. Goliath and his personal keeper, James Bargantine, arrived from Atlantic City where they were employed by Ringling Brothers Circus, which had rented space from the Zoo to accommodate Goliath for the winter. Unlike Leo, Goliath only remained at the Zoo a matter of months, but in those months the mammoth seventeen-foot-long southern sea elephant had more photos of his image published in local and national newspapers than most zoo animals would ever accomplish in a lifetime. In fact, a Zoological Society history of the Zoo, *An Animal Garden in Fairmount Park*, published in 1988, features a cover photo of Goliath and Bargantine—a couple of day-trippers when compared with keep-ers like John McMullen, who by 1933 was a fifty-year veteran at the Zoo, or Thomas B. Manley, head keeper of the Zoo from 1891 to 1922, whose ashes were buried on the Zoo grounds after his death in 1939. As you can see by the size of Goliath's mouth, he had quite an appetite and he exercised it every day, gobbling down a barrel of fish at each feeding. His accommodations were—suitably or ironically—in the outdoor pool used by the elephants to bathe in the summer. Goliath spent most of his time at the bottom of the pool sleeping and awaiting his next meal. Since he had to come up every now and then for air, during freezing weather, night watchmen had to make the rounds ever hour or so to crack any ice that would have formed over his air hole. Goliath was on the market but the Zoo had no money during the Depression to purchase him, and the public had no money to pay admission to the Zoo to visit him. He left the Zoo in April of 1934, but his photos live on.

Goliath at feeding time.

Monkey Island and the Great Escapes

There have only been two mass breakouts of animals in Zoo history, both of them involving the residents of Monkey Island. Built in 1938 with WPA funding, Monkey Island consisted of a mountain of rocks cemented together and rising from the middle of a concrete bowl that was filled with water to create a moat that prevented the monkeys from escaping. At least in theory.

Monkey Island was a very popular exhibit. Every year at the beginning of each spring season thirty young rhesus monkeys would be released from a trapdoor on the island connected to a tunnel underneath. The monkeys would then have the island with its sliding board, seesaw, rope swings, and other playground equipment to themselves.

In the early years the release of the monkeys onto Monkey Island took place during the May Day celebration, the Zoo's heavily promoted first Sunday in May, when upwards of twenty thousand visitors flocked to the Zoo. After one such May Day in 1940, the moat around Monkey Island had to be drained because of all the bottles and other trash that had been thrown into it by thoughtless people. It was a Monday morning, and Roger Conant was sitting at his desk when the first newspaper called asking about two escaped monkeys near Thirty-fourth Street and

A young rhesus monkey, AWOL from the Philadelphia Zoo, took refuge on the huge equestrian statue of George Washington in front of the Philadelphia Museum of Art in May 1945. At top is one of the firemen who assisted zookeepers in capturing the runaway.

Photo by Jack Snyder, courtesy of the *Philadelphia Record*.

boys, presumably, tossed into the moat on Monkey Island. Nineteen of the twenty-five monkeys on the island escaped, running out the South Gate past a startled ticket taker. This time they took up positions in the trees on the other side of Thirty-fourth Street between the Zoo and West River Drive. It was much harder to get the monkeys down from the trees than rooftops, and zookeepers had to wait them out until they got hungry and returned to the Zoo looking for food. One monkey did venture back to the scene of the first Great Escape on the row house rooftops of Mantua. It was captured after a long chase by three zookeepers. It ran into an open hatch on a rooftop into a crawl space above a bedroom. The smallest keeper climbed in after it, and a few moments later, keeper, monkey, plaster, and lathe tumbled from the ceiling onto a bed adjacent to where a young girl was taking a nap. The Zoo paid for the damage.

The final monkey was caught days later after being spotted on top of George Washington's hat on the statue of Washington astride a horse in front of the Philadelphia Museum of Art. The monkey had evidently crossed the Spring Garden Street Bridge and sought high ground on the Washington Monument. Firemen climbed ladders onto the statue in pursuit of the monkey, and a front page photo appeared in the next day's *Philadelphia Record*. Still, the monkey eluded capture, until sheer exhaustion overtook it. It sat down on the grass to rest and a passerby picked it up and presented it to the zookeepers.

Mantua Avenue. The next newspaper to call reported five monkeys. By the time the *Daily News* called the number of escapees was up to one hundred.

Actually, it was only fifteen, but it seemed like one hundred, scampering over rooftops and fences and trees in the residential neighborhood on the south side of the railroad tracks. Zookeepers, police, and a posse of volunteers began rounding up the monkeys. The first one returned to the Zoo, immediately escaped again, and in the process demonstrated how the monkeys had broken out by leaping onto a drain pipe from the bottom of the empty moat and then leaped again to the top. The first Great Escape attracted hundreds of sightseers, including children returning home for lunch from the nearby Morton McMichael (former mayor and an original Zoo founder) School. One lady fainted when a monkey jumped from a second-story roof and hit the pavement (she thought it was dead, but it wasn't even hurt). Another monkey was cornered by the amateur zookeepers on a rooftop, where it leaped down a chimney and suffocated. One monkey peeked in on a woman taking a bath, nearly scaring her to death. Another was captured in a delicatessen behind a pickle barrel.

That first Great Escape from Monkey Island knocked Hitler's advance through Belgium and Holland off the front pages that day. A downward tilting cover was placed over the drainpipe to prevent future escapes, and none took place until Hitler was in his bunker just days from Germany's defeat in May 1945. Once again it happened on a Monday following opening day. This time the means of escape was wooden planks used the day before to build a stage, which workmen had disassembled and which mischievous teenage

Monkey Island on May Day 1954.

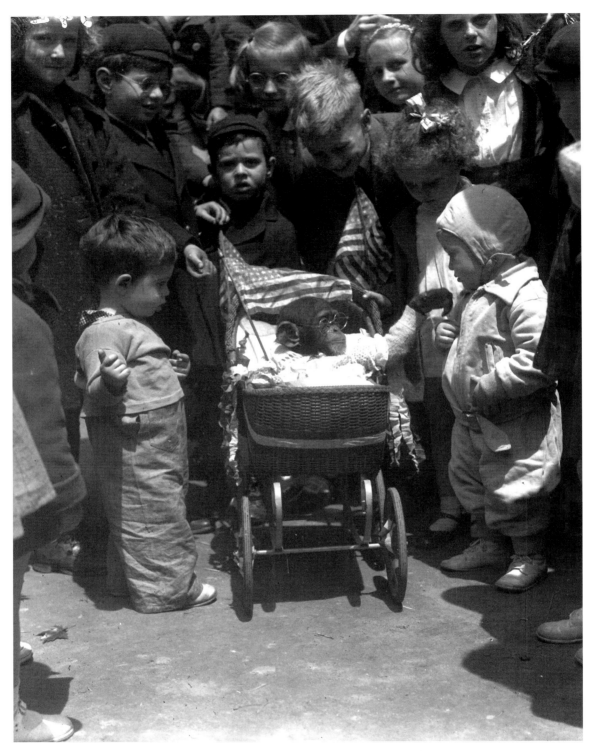

Children and patriotic chimp commune at the Baby Pet Zoo.

THE WAR YEARS AND BEYOND ZOOSTORY

By 1940 the Great Depression had become life as usual. Philadelphians were so used to belt tightening and economic hard times that the city's ribs were showing. That year's census revealed something that hadn't happened since William Penn landed on the Delaware River shore of his "green country town" in 1683— Philadelphia actually lost population. This was a Depression-era phenomenon that would foreshadow the postwar depopulation of most older American cities (Philadelphia's population didn't peak until 1950). But declining birth rates and lack of job opportunities for natives, let alone immigrants, led to the first ten-year loss of population in the city, from 1,950,961 reported in the 1930 census to 1,931,334 in 1940. Although the city lost 50,000 whites during that period, the net loss was only 19,000 because of an increase of 31,000 blacks, who now represented 13 percent of Philadelphia's total population.

By 1940 the New Deal make-work bureaucracy was entrenched and active. WPA could have stood for We'll Pave Anything, and the zoo was the beneficiary of a number of public works projects generated by the federal government, including the construction of the Baby Pet Zoo and Monkey Island in 1938. WPA workers were employed during the construction in 1940 of the new Pachyderm House, a massive structure of solid stone designed by Zoo architect Paul Cret in the style of a Pennsylvania Dutch barn, complete with

the same time the number of visitors had increased from an annual low of 152,096 in 1932 to a respectable 333,598 in 1940. It wasn't the size of the collection that drew visitors as much as the overall *experience* during a visit to the Zoo, and the physical improvements made to the garden during the 1930s enhanced that experience.

In 1940 the storm clouds of war in Europe led to the first peacetime draft in American history. In that same year 91,000 foreign-born Philadelphians registered their whereabouts with the government under the Alien Registration Act, leading to FBI raids on homes, workplaces, and German or Italian social clubs. In 1940, the corruption-plagued Philadelphia Rapid Transit Company (PRT) became the strike-plagued (eight strikes in twenty-eight years) Philadelphia Transportation Company (PTC), a private-public entity that would become SEPTA in 1968. Nineteen-forty was the year Marian Anderson won the Philadelphia Award. It was also the year the Republican National Convention met in Philadelphia to nominate Wendell

hex sign. The old Elephant House built in 1875 stood where the Lion House stands today. Funding for the new Pachyderm House, which has stood up to the constant trampings of both man and beast for six decades, was part of a generous bequest from former Zoo Director Wilson Catherwood. That same bequest paid for the construction of the Zoo's desperately needed Service Building, which was completed in 1938 and which bears Catherwood's name.

The Zoo had emerged from the decade of the Depression much like the city itself—with fewer permanent citizens. The number of animals in the collection had been reduced from an unmanageable high of over 3,000 in the early 1930s to a total of 1,781 in 1940. At

Williams B. Cadwalader mans a shovel at the groundbreaking for the new Pachyderm House in March 1940. Also included in the party are Paul Cret, R. Sturgis Ingersoll, Freeman Shelly, and the contractor.

Wilkie as the candidate to stop Franklin Roosevelt from being elected for an unprecedented third term as president. Another lasting legacy from 1940 was an act by City Council creating the Philadelphia Wage Tax at a modest rate of 1.5 percent.

The Great Depression ended the instant the first Japanese bomb landed on the American fleet in Pearl Harbor. Philadelphians were eating their dinners on December 7, 1941, when the news arrived from the Hawaiian Islands. By the next day there were long lines of young men outside draft boards, and Philadelphia industry, as if one great switch turned on a gigantic

Bombing raid sharpshooters exhibit on May Day 1942.

engine, came alive. For the second time in the not-yet-half-completed century, Philadelphia changed from describing itself as "Workshop of the World" to "Arsenal of America" to meet the needs of a global conflict. More than a billion dollars worth of government contracts poured into Philadelphia industries from shipyards to paper mills. The Franklin Arsenal produced thousands of .75 millimeter recoilless rifles, Philco produced radar bombsights, Rohm and Haas manufactured plexiglass for bomber turrets, Cramps reopened shipyard turned out submarines and flying boats. The city went back to work with a vengeance. Philadelphians also went to war in staggering numbers. By 1945 there were 183,850 men and women from Philadelphia in uniform.

At the Zoo, the war was both a boon and a bother. Some of the Zoo's best employees enlisted and it was difficult to find replacements in the suddenly depleted labor market. At the same time that jobs went unfilled at the Zoo, attendance soared just as it had during World War I. More visitors and fewer employees meant more work for an increasingly aged staff. On top of that there was rationing, shortages of supplies, disruptions caused by air-raid drills and special precautions required in case enemy bombers managed to damage structures holding dangerous

His number came up and he has to go like anyone else.

Cartoon from Zoo News, *March 1943.*

animals (sharpshooters were designated with orders to shoot any escaped animal).

Patriotic fervor took many shapes. On the positive side a Victory garden was planted on a 26,000-square-foot parcel of land where the old Elephant House had been and the vegetables grown there fed the Zoo stock. During the popular May Day festivities in 1942 programs were designed around wartime themes such as "Weapons of the Wild," featuring the natural weapons and defensive capabilities of animals that are similar to modern weaponry (hippos for submarines, porcupines for barbed wire, rhinos for armored tanks, and skunks for poison gas). On the

Copyright © by Steve Walker.

zoos. London's animals survived unscathed, but German zoos suffered terrible losses, not so much from ordinance dropped by enemy aircraft as much as starvation and neglect. In the Zoo's magazine *Fauna*, Zoo staffers serving overseas reported on the conditions in zoos in liberated cities like Antwerp, Paris, and Rome, as well as in defeated cities like Berlin, Nuremberg, and Munich. "Adolf should see the place now. It's a mess!" wrote Corporal Robert Hudson about the Munich Zoo, where he found Polish slave laborers tending to the animals.

Despite gasoline rationing that all but eliminated pleasure driving, Philadelphians swarmed to the Zoo during the war. Attendance rose from 400,000 in 1941 to 500,000 in 1945 and 670,000 the following year. The annual May Day celebrations drew huge crowds. May Day 1943 saw a crowd of almost 40,000 paying customers pass through the gates, and since servicemen in uniform were admitted free, the actual number of visitors was even larger. Zoogoers depended on public transportation, as did everyone else, and in August 1944 the transportation workers union called a strike against the PTC after black employees were

A crowd awaits entry at the North Gate on May Day 1945.

negative side of patriotism, animals identified with America's wartime enemies were subject to abuse. Japanese macaque monkeys were pelted with stones on one occasion, and the signs identifying Japanese sika deer were destroyed. During World War I precautions against just such misguided acts of brutality or vandalism were taken, especially in the case of the Indian elephant purchased in Hamburg in 1902. In 1917 after fifteen years at the Zoo, the elephant named Kaiserine was rechristened Lizzie to avoid arousing anti-German passions.

Bombs never fell on Philadelphia's Zoo, but they did fall in London, Berlin, and other European city

promoted (due to manpower shortages) to the positions of conductor and motorman. President Roosevelt ordered federal troops to Philadelphia to keep the important war production industries running by making sure workers had transportation to and from work. For ten days until the strike ended armed soldiers with fixed bayonets rode trolleys as black conductors took tickets.

During the war the Zoo enlisted its services on behalf of American servicemen who were being bitten by poisonous snakes while on maneuvers at Army camps throughout the United States. The only U.S. manufacturer of anti-venin for rattlesnake venom was Sharp and Dohme Laboratories in Glenolden, and the Philadelphia Zoo's Reptile Department took over the task of collecting and then milking poisonous domestic snakes to provide the venom necessary to create the antidote serum. A poison cocktail of venoms from copperheads, water moccasins, and a variety of rattlesnakes was mixed together and injected into a horse in ever-increasing doses. Once the horse could withstand a fatal dose of venom, an anti-venin serum was made from its blood. The Zoo's assistant curator of reptiles, Nigel Wolff, was in charge of the Snake House at Glenolden. On December 9, 1943, Wolff was dispatched from the Zoo with ampules of cobra anti-venin after a boy in Red Bank, New Jersey, was bitten by a deadly coral snake that the boy's father had received from a soldier overseas. Wolff took the train to Trenton where a State Police car waited to rush him to the hospital where fourteen-year-old Fred Wege lay dying. A total of five cobra anti-venin ampules were injected over the course of several hours and the boy was declared out of danger the next day. The Zoo had received the precious anti-venin from the Pasteur Institute in Paris shortly before the Nazis occupied that city.

The war effectively halted all importation of animals from Asia, Africa, and Australia. The last exotic animals to make it to Philadelphia during the war were two giraffes from Kenya, who arrived on May 5, 1942, on a ship that was fired upon by a German submarine and stopped by a German surface boat before being rescued by allied destroyers. Nineteen-forty-three was a bad year, starting with an outbreak of botulism on Bird Lake that killed twenty-four ducks and geese. In a matter of months during 1943, more than a dozen of the Zoo's oldest and most beloved animals died of natural causes and accidents. Among them were Josephine the Indian elephant that had carried 175,000 Zoo visitors on her back during her eighteen years at the Zoo before dying of a heart attack on May 12, 1943. A month earlier Peggy the Indian rhino died of renal failure. Peggy had been captured in the wild twenty years earlier by the famous pith-helmeted animal collector Frank "Bring 'Em Back Alive" Buck. Also dying were the thirty-nine-year-old European pelican following an accident that broke its wing, a thirty-four-year-old griffin vulture that strangled on its food, and a twenty-nine-year-old dromedary that died of natural causes, as did a crocodile, a goliath heron, and a rosie-billed duck. Ironically, one of the giraffes that had survived the torpedoes during the transatlantic crossing was found dead on September 3, 1943, of a fractured skull. Zoo officials suspect that the dead giraffe, Jane, had been accidentally kicked in the head by her mate, Jim.

Pharmacists Mate First Class Robert E. Wright poses with his coati-mundi in 1945.

Restocking the Zoo depended on trades with other North American zoos, but returning servicemen proved to an unexpected source of several new additions to the collection. Pharmacists Mate First Class Robert E. Wright of Margate, New Jersey, presented the Zoo with a coati-mundi he'd purchased for a dollar and kept on shipboard as a pet. When he returned to Margate (possibly at the bidding of Lucy the Elephant) Wright decided that the Zoo was a better home for the animal. Ack-Ack, an Indian crow named for the noise it makes, arrived in Philadelphia with a merchant seaman who left it in payment at a waterfront taproom. The bar owner kept it for two months, then gave it to the Zoo saying, "He eats nothing but hamburgers and he doesn't have any ration points." In September 1945 a returning GI from Massachusetts presented the Zoo with a Barbary ape from Gibraltar after writing to the Zoo that he had heard about Philadelphia's "unusual success in keeping apes and monkeys." By 1945,

Bamboo, the Zoo's nineteen-year-old gorilla was world famous for his long life in captivity. And waiting in the wings to establish another record for gorilla longevity was Massa.

During the war the Zoo refused to answer questions from the public about which countries were home to certain animals because sometimes GIs wrote home describing animals they'd seen. After a few such calls the Zoo called Army Intelligence and asked what response they should give to such queries. "Tell them nothing," the Army ordered. "There are plenty of enemy agents around and, if they learn where one man is, it often identifies his regiment or division." The Zoo suffered several human casualties among the staff and members who served in uniform. Fireman Second Class Joseph Hough, who worked at the Zoo Restaurant, was killed at Normandy. Alan Dougal Jones, past secretary of the Junior Zoological Society, was killed in action during the Battle of the Bulge. And Ted Bunalski, another

This Barbary ape was donated to the Zoo in 1945.

Junior Zoological Society member, died while fighting a fire on a bomber in England. Winners of the Purple Heart were Pat Menichini, Lion House keeper, who suffered a chest wound and then Private Hudson, of the Zoo's Graphics Department, who suffered a leg injury.

Plans for the postwar Zoo were underway well before the invasion of Normandy. Zoo Director Freeman Shelly filed documents with the Philadelphia Planning Commission detailing four projects that would be the centerpiece of a six-year postwar improvement plan. They included the construction of a Lion and Tiger House with cageless grottos, as well as a connecting building to hold smaller cats such as leopards, pumas, and ocelots. Plans were made for a Great Ape House on the site of the old Lion House (the Rare Animal House today) as well as a new Monkey Island adjacent to the new Primate House. Of the four, only the new Monkey Island never materialized.

The end of World War II brought a new era to the Zoo, which at seventy-one years old was looking every bit its age. In a nuclear age, the nineteenth-century Victorian ideal of caged animals in rigid alignment seemed both antiquated and cruel. The Zoo's president, Dr. Williams Cadwalader, declared the majority of Zoo buildings to be "ugly, unsanitary and unsafe" not to mention "outmoded and evil-smelling." Cadwalader rallied support from Philadelphia politicians and on August 1, 1946, Mayor Bernard Samuel, the city's last Republican mayor of the century, announced that the city was committing one million dollars to capital improvements—this from a city administration that barely a dozen years before cut its annual appropriation for the Zoo from $50,000 to $25,000.

The first reinforcements in the animal collection at the war-depleted Zoo arrived in 1946 in a shipment from the London Zoo of one hundred mammals, birds, and reptiles who made the sixteen-day ocean crossing under the care of First Sergeant Fred Ulmer, the newly appointed curator of mammals, who did everything from preparing the food to cleaning the cages during the stormy voyage.

It was during the immediate postwar period that the Zoo was blessed with the arrival of philanthropist angels like South Philadelphia restaurateur Frank Palumbo who began hosting an annual outing at the Zoo for thousands of underprivileged children, at which time he inevitably donated an animal to the collection. In 1947 it was a leopard named Chief. This was followed by a hippo, an eagle, several penguins,

Elephants perform at the May Day celebration in 1942.

May Day Poster, 1941.

and most significantly, a pair of rare black rhinoceroses in 1948.

The first year after the end of the war, the Zoo flirted with breaking its one year attendance record set in the Centennial year of 1876 when 677,630 visitors passed through the gates. The total for 1946 fell short of breaking the record by under 2,000. But it was an indication of what was to come in the years ahead. Admission to the Zoo was still only thirty-five cents for adults and twenty cents for children under twelve (children under five were free), and the bargain was not lost on prospective visitors even after admission prices for adults were jacked up to fifty cents in 1948. The Zoo found another means of augmenting income when it started allowing the public to feed the sea lions for a nickel a fish beginning in August 1948. The public simply threw the fish to the sea lions at feeding time until the daily quota of fish was gone. Such brilliant cost-effective marketing was a sign that the Zoo was gathering momentum for its Diamond Jubilee in 1949, the celebration of the opening of America's first zoo seventy-five years earlier.

Left:
Santa Claus feeds the reindeer in December 1942.

Below:
Carmichael the polar bear hangs out by his pool in 1942.

Photo by Kauffeld.

California sea lion at feeding time.

PET BANK
BORROW ANIMALS HERE

Pet Bank, 1942.

Black bear cubs Roosevelt and Churchill, April 1943.

Baby skunks Hitler and Mussolini were born on May 2, 1945.

Ostrich with keepers.

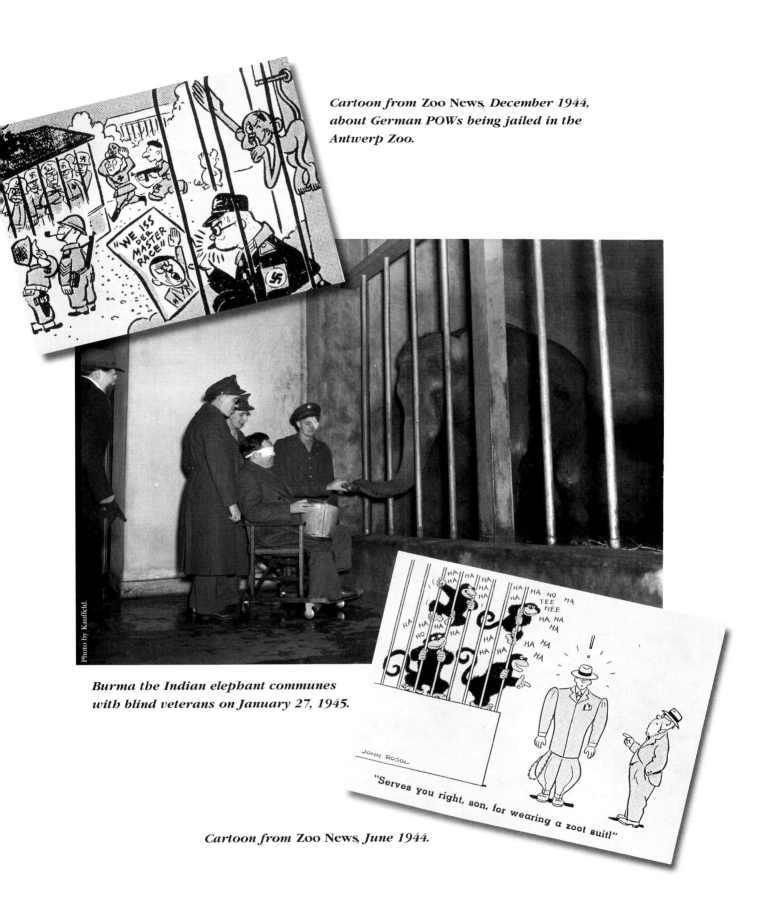

Cartoon from Zoo News, December 1944, about German POWs being jailed in the Antwerp Zoo.

Burma the Indian elephant communes with blind veterans on January 27, 1945.

Photo by Kauffeld.

JOHN ROSOL

"Serves you right, son, for wearing a zoot suit!"

Cartoon from Zoo News, June 1944.

Photo by Kauffeld.

Left:
This Zoo exhibit was in Fairmount Park at the Fourth of July party hosted by the Evening Bulletin *in 1946.*

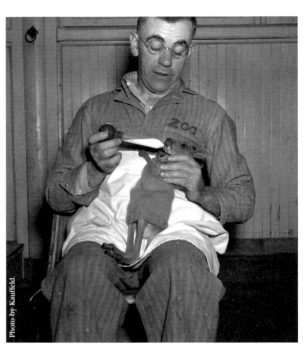

Photo by Kauffeld.

Right:
John Regan feeds a baby kangaroo in 1944.

Below:
Operation on a python to remove a neck tumor in 1946.

Photo by Kauffeld.

News photographers focus on the feeding of the seal.

Note the "kid" at the middle left in this Pet Zoo grandstand crowd.

Above:

No one loved the Zoo more than Frank Palumbo, the South Philadelphia restauranteur who lent this side of his property at Ninth and Catherine Streets to promote the Zoo in 1949.

Below:

F. Robert Gilpin feeds Burma the Indian elephant in February 1949.

A banner promoting the Zoo hangs across Market Street in downtown Philadelphia in May 1948.

Trolley poster from April 1949.

Left:
Zoo staffers pose in their costumes for Old Timers' Day in June 1949 to celebrate the Zoo's seventy-fifth anniversary.

The cornerstone for the new Lion House was laid in 1949. Included in this photo are Mayor Bernard Samuel, Williams B. Cadwalader, John Regan, Pat Menichini, Pandora the chimp, and an unidentified lion cub.

Photo by Isabelle Hunt.

Jeepers Keepers

"There are no second chances on this job," says Steve Cepregi, the head lion keeper. He speaks for all the keepers at the Zoo because that is a phrase you hear over and over, almost like a mantra. Animals are dangerous, not because they are evil, but because they are wild. They can be trained, but never tamed. And never confuse the difference between the two.

"One time I tried to give up coffee," Susie Gurley, head tiger keeper, recalls one morning six years ago, "and I stumbled against a cage and a puma reached out with its paw and clawed me on the hand. It happened just like that. The claw pierced my hand and went straight through the other side. I grabbed its paw and pulled my hand free before it could tear away the flesh. I never tried to give up coffee again."

What can bug keepers?

"Put in the book that we really hate it when people say, 'What kind of animal is that?' when we're inside a cage cleaning it," says Susie.

Steve has a standard reply to that question, "I tell them that I'm an imperial crested visitor killer."

Another thing that bugs keepers is when visitors ask questions while the keepers are working with the animals. "It's a very stressful job," says Susie, "Especially when the public is interrupting you."

Says Steve, "You'll be in the middle of doing something and someone will say something to you, and all of a sudden you're thinking, 'Did I lock that door? Did I leave it open?' It can be unnerving."

And then there are the visitors who taunt the animals. "I give a speech about the difference between being a keeper and being kept," says Steve. "Sometimes the public can be clueless about how dangerous these cats are. I've seen parents hold their kids up in front of the cage and say, "Watch it, the lion's gonna get you" and then

There are no second chances.

dangle the child in front of the lion. It's hard to believe."

It's also hard to believe what is said by people who really should know better. Scott Bartow, monkey keeper in the Rare Animal House, shakes his head at what a teacher once said to her class in front of Scott. The school group stopped in front of the cage that Scott was cleaning, and the teachers turned to the children and said, "See what happens if you don't get a good education. You end up with a job like that!"

"I've heard amazing things, good and bad, out of all kinds of people," says Julie Unger-Smith, primate keeper.

What do keepers fear most?

"I have a nightmare about Lantar [the male tiger] getting loose," says Susie Gurley. "I have this dream about the cage fronts just falling down. I never dream that I'm killed, but that I'm responsible for another keeper being killed." Oddly enough, it's not the public that zookeepers imagine being hurt by the animals as much as it is the staff. "Why is it that the public never gets hurt and it's always the keepers," asks Lynn Fulton the head elephant keeper. "Ever notice that? Whenever there's a problem, like if a kid falls in or something, they never get hurt. I've never seen anyone but keepers get hurt, and I've seen lots of people jump these barriers and touch them. And the elephants never hurt them. It's probably because the elephants are looking for food and those people are no threats to them. They don't give them orders, they don't tell them what to do.

Sara Cunius and Indian cobra in 1953.

We're the ones who are endangered. We're the ones who lock them up everyday and tell them what to do."

What's the biggest change at the Zoo over the years?

"The biggest change in all the thirty-five years I've been here has been the philosophy of zoos," says Steve Cepregi. "There's a lot more concern about the animal's well being. Back in the sixties I called these [lion cages] toilets. There was nothing to them. No balls for them to play with. No climbing branches. Nothing that we call enrichment today."

What's the best part of the job?

"Being close to the animals," says Steve. "It's so cool. We feel that every day. You never lose that." Susie agrees. And that's one aspect of having animals behind bars that is lost to the public when the same animals are seen on the other side of a moat, like when Lantar walks out of his indoor cage into his barred outdoor enclosure. "There's something about being that close and breathing the same air," she says. The often cantankerous but lovable head keeper at the Bird House, Sonny Woerner, puts it another way, "If you don't like animals you shouldn't work at the Zoo," Sonny says. "Otherwise it's just a job. You're just working for the money."

"People have often said to me about working in the Zoo, 'You're not in the real world,'" says Julie Unger-Smith. "You come to the gate and you're in this, well, it's not Disney World but it's darn close. It's not meant to be Disney World, but it's not the real world either. It's a little chunk of land where so many good things are happening in the midst of so many bad things we see every day. It's a kind of a hope. And it's bigger than ourselves. And it's something that's going to go on, I hope, forever."

A white tiger relaxes in the Carnivora House's outdoor grotto.

ZOOMSTORY TO THE NINETIES

PHILADELPHIA

AMERICA'S FIRST ZOO

America's first zoostory begins to fast forward in the nuclear age. Ideas changed rapidly about the way animals should be displayed, and whether they should be on display in the first place. In the fifty years between the Diamond Jubilee of 1949 to the Quasquicentennial of 1999, the Zoo developed in ways parallel to, and sometimes completely opposite from the city around it. Like the city itself, the Zoo entered an ambitious building period in the early 1950s. You could compare the construction of the Carnivora House with its outdoor grottos for lions and tigers with the demolition of the Chinese Wall (the massive Pennsylvania Railroad viaduct that ran from City Hall to Thirtieth Street) and the construction of Penn Center. You could also compare how quickly both completed projects fell into disfavor among critics. The Carnivora House, built with city money, opened with high praise as the being the best in the world in 1951, yet in a matter of years it was seen as unnatural, antiseptic, prison-like, and worst of all, old-fashioned. Penn Center was a stunningly ambitious urban renewal project that transformed a section of crumbling Center City, and yet public enthusiasm began to turn critical when the first colorless boxy office towers were completed, defining a new Center City of windy plazas devoid of people and street life.

Yet unlike the city's population trend during the fifties, sixties, and seventies the Zoo's attendance grew steadily during the decades that followed. Philadelphia reached its peak population of 2,071,605 in the 1950 census when it still ranked third largest of American cities, rather than fifth. Of that number 1,692,637 Philadelphians were white, and the city's black population of 376,041 was 18 percent of the total. The rapid decline in white population (by 1970 there were 410,000 fewer whites) corresponded with increasing numbers of blacks (by 1970 there were 323,000 more blacks, 33.6 percent of the total). The worst of the white flight had ended by the end of the 1980s. The 1990 census shows a population of 1,585,577, with declines in both the city's white and black population. The projected population for the 2000 census—1,513,674—shows the smallest decline in decades.

During the same year, annual attendance at the Zoo, which had putt-putted along in the two-to-four hundred thousand range for most of its prior history, began to climb steadily as the city's population dwindled. In 1951, the Zoo broke a seventy-five-year-old attendence record of 677,630 established during the U.S. Centennial year of 1876. Attracted by the opening of the new Carnivora House, 857,901 visitors passed through the Zoo gates. That record fell six

Entrance to the Children's Zoo, July 1957.

years later with the opening of the Daniel W. Dietrich Memorial Children's Zoo—the first children's zoo in the country—when attendance reached 874,351. "The Philadelphia Zoo attracts more persons than any of our other cultural institutions," an emboldened Zoo Director Freeman Shelly told the Citizens Council on City Planning in 1960. "In fact, from a standpoint of attendance, we are exceeded only by the Phillies baseball club, and if some of the deals for players, which they made recently, do not work out, we shall go ahead of them." It would take another six years for the Zoo to crack the million barrier. It happened on November 1, 1966, when Margaret Serino, an eleven-year-old from Prospect Park, New Jersey, was identified as the first one-millionth visitor of the year at America's first zoo. Since then the Zoo has attracted over a million visitors annually, with the next yet-to-be-broken attendance goal being 1.5 million.

H. Richard Dietrich, Williams B. Cadwalader, and orangutan at the presentation of a gift to the new Children's Zoo in March 1957.

A Zoo-Illogical Star

It's very hard to think of a less likely animal star at the Zoo than Prickly Pete. When he died on March 18, 1953, Prickly Pete had been living at the Zoo longer than any other animal, just seven months shy of fifty years. And most people do not think of echidnas in terms of longevity. Most people don't think of echidnas at all, unless they confuse them with something on a Mexican restaurant menu. Enchiladas, echidnas, whatever. Actually, echidnas are small egg-laying mammals resembling hedgehogs and related to the platypus. They also like to sleep during the day which makes them just about perfect for *not* attracting the attention of visitors, who couldn't see Prickly Pete anyway because he lived in a darkened box in the Small Mammal House. Only upon request would a keeper lift up the lid of the box so that a visitor could watch it sleep.

But during his half century at the Zoo, Prickly Pete (he only rated a name after reaching the age of forty. Up until then he was simply "the echidna") got more press than most animals. His longevity, plus his daily diet of exactly one raw egg and exactly one pint of milk served in separate pans every day of his life at the Zoo, seemed to get mentioned in some publication at least once every year until that inevitable day when a keeper lifted the lid of his box to discover, alas, that Pete was no longer prickling with us. After his death, the Zoo announced the results of the post-mortem. "The autopsy showed that Patricia would have been a better name," the Zoo magazine reported. "After fifty years, Prickly Pete turned out to be a lady. Who says a woman doesn't know how to keep a secret?"

Left:
Front of Small Mammal House.

Below:
Rare Animal House, center view, 1965.

This is not Prickly Pete, but for those who are unfamiliar with the animal, this is a short-beaked echidna.

During the fifties and sixties close to half of the aging buildings in the Zoo were either rebuilt or totally renovated. The Bird House built in 1916 was gutted, expanded, and remodeled. The old Reptile House and Small Mammal House were subject to three-quarters of a million dollars worth of improvements. The old Lion House built in 1873 was torn down and replaced with the new Rare Mammal House which opened in 1965.

Freeman Shelly, the director of the Zoo since the grim days of the Depression, chose the end of the Zoo's first million-visitor year to retire on a high note in 1966 after thirty years. He had served under two legendary chairmen of the Board of Directors, Williams B. Cadwalader, whose fifty-one years on the Board (1906 to 1957) is a record as safe from being broken as Joe DiMaggio's fifty-six-game hitting streak, and Radcliffe Cheston, Jr., whose forty years on the Board (1928 to 1968) places him in a second-place tie with an earlier forty-year Board veteran and former chairman, Christian C. Febiger. There are a number of three-decade-plus Board members in the Society's history, including the famous novelist Owen Wister, author of *The Virginian*.

Shelly, a formal man, was replaced by Roger Conant, who was not. Given to wearing cowboy hats and bolo ties, Conant was already a legend in American zoology when he took over the president's

John A. "Gus" Griswald, curator of birds.

office in *Solitude*—a name he discovered that suits the job. Conant, a tireless writer, promoter, and cheerleader for the Zoo, was also an internationally reknown herpetologist, and in fact is the only person ever employed at the Zoo to discover a species and have it named after him, *Lampropeltis Triangulum Conanti*, Conant's milksnake. He had been curator of reptiles since 1936, and was one of the most popular people at the Zoo. Upon becoming president, Conant found out why people say it's lonely at the top. "An unexpected phenomenon surfaced immediately after I took office, when a number of employees exhibited

Docent Council. Back row, left to right, are Phyllis Morrison, Marilyn O'Neill, Kathryn Marshall, Susan Kaplan, Winnie Schilling, Carolyn Willms, Barbara Pruyn, Charlotte Powel, and Barbara Nolan. In the middle row are Dorothy Szabody, Lois Abendroth, Janet Yudkin, Doris Guttentag, Esther Linville, Betty Grieb, and Louise Bordibn. In front are Janet Wilson, Carole Ashmead, and Marilyn Hill.

wrote. "Now as I walked around the Zoo, they turned their backs on me. I tried to start conversations with some of them, but their response was stoney silence." Conant later discovered that this was a union-ordered tactic involving an ongoing labor dispute, but it set the tone for Conant's tenure as director. His chapter on becoming Zoo director is titled, "The Difficult Years."

New construction continued at the Zoo under Conant, including the much needed (and now woefully inadequate) Educational/Administration Building that bears Shelly's name and opened in 1972. Plans for the first phase of the African Plains Exhibit, and the Eleanor S. Gray Hummingbird Exhibit were underway. It was during Conant's directorship that the Zoo's inimitable Docent Council was founded in 1971 by the even more inimitable Jeanne Segal and Virginia Pearson. The docents are undoubtedly the most knowledgeable group of Zoo volunteers. After completing a Green Berets level of classroom and on-site training about the Zoo, the new docents are then allowed to don their silver wings—or in the case of docents, don their yellow sashes—identifying them as Zoo guides.

Conant retired in 1973 and his successor, Ronald Reuther, director of the San Francisco Zoo, served in the top post during the Zoo's Centennial Celebration year of 1974. There were mummers, there were parties, there were speeches galore. Phase One of the African Plains Exhibit opened amid much fanfare. Phase One had been designed by Henry Mirick, a Zoo Board member, whose plan disguised the holding barns for giraffes, zebras, elands, and warthogs behind a rock cliff facade made of Gunite. It's fun for visitors to try to spot the hidden doors the animals use to come and go. One continuing legacy of the celebration of the Centennial year is Zoobilee, which was born in 1974 and which has become the annual party-nobody-wants-to-miss. Board Chairman John Williams dubbed the outdoor bash Zoobilee, and over the years it has provided a

Chuck Ripka and Dan Maloney display elephant keepers' equipment at Zoobilee in 1989.

a marked change in attitude toward me," Conant wrote in his autobiography about his years as director. Old friends no longer sought him out. "I was now the boss instead of a confidant." He also discovered something about labor relations. "For years I had been friendly with virtually all of the employees," he number of people an opportunity to become involved with the Zoo on more than a social and volunteer basis. Current Board Chairman Barry C. Lyngard cites the fun he and his wife had at their first Zoobilee as his real introduction to the Zoo. The road to his becoming chairman of the Board started with he and his wife being asked to volunteer to lick stamps for Zoobilee mailings. "Up to that point, I hadn't been able or in a position to give something back," Lyngard said.

In 1976, the Zoo's record-setting female orangutan, Guarina, died at the age of fifty-six, and a year later she was joined by her mate, Guas. The pair had held the world record for longest-living non-human primates. In 1977, ground was broken for Bear Country on the site of the original Bear Pits from 1874. When it opened three years later, the Polar Bear Exhibit with its huge glass underwater viewing area was a smash hit. The Zoo ran print advertisements much like the movie ad for *Jaws*, showing the polar bear rising in the water under the headline, "Paws."

In 1977, John A. "Gus" Griswald, the Zoo's widely respected curator of birds, announced his retirement after thirty years. His success in the captive rearing of trumpeter swans in the United States was hailed by the U.S. Department of Interior. At the end of the year, Board Chairman John W. York announced the resignation of Ronald Reuther, whose four-year directorship was one of the shortest in Zoo history.

After a nationwide search that continued for a full year and a half, during which the Zoo was administered by Acting Director Dr. Wilbur Amand, the Board announced its selection for the new Zoo president—not director. His name was William V. Donaldson, and he was unlike anyone the Zoo or Philadelphia had seen before. Donaldson, a large, loud, white-haired teddy bear of a man had been city manager of Cincinnati when he accepted the Zoo post. He had

Phase one of the African Plains Exhibit.

had a lifelong love affair with animals and zoos, and he immediately poured that enthusiasm, administrative ability, and natural showmanship into his new job. He quickly became not only one of the most recognizable figures at the Zoo, but also in the entire city because Donaldson was the Will Rogers of microphones—he never met one he didn't like. Under Donaldson, the Zoo's educational mission was expanded into an entire department which today is involved in an almost inexhaustible number of programs and projects that take the Zoo to the schools, as well as take students to the Zoo or wildlife preserves or, as they did last summer, took seven students to Kenya.

The pipe-smoking Donaldson was a born schmoozer. Unlike previous Zoo directors, he could talk with ease and effectiveness to maintenance workers, labor leaders, curators, keepers, politicians, wealthy donors, and the news media. His spirit and personality solved a number of disputes that would have flared into confrontations under someone else's less nimble touch. Donaldson loved animals, loved being with animals, loved talking about animals. But he left the important decisions about animals to Karl Kranz and other members of the Animal Department.

*Pandora the chimp at the Zoo's
1950 Christmas party.*

Treehouse.

Animal was bringing in $215,000 per year. Corporate donations were minimal in 1980—zero, actually. By 1987, corporate donors had been tapped to the tune of $205,000. Private donations increased from $350,000 in 1979 to $2.1 million in 1987 to $5.39 million in 1999. Donaldson was the Ed Rendell of the Philadelphia Zoo. What you saw was what you got: cheerleader, numbers cruncher, savvy administrator, straight talker, visionary, conversationalist, regular guy.

Under Donaldson, the Zoo saw the construction of the hugely successful Treehouse in the old Antelope House, as well as the World of Primates and Carnivore Kingdom. It was "P. T. Barnum" Donaldson who knew what would bring people into the tent. One year it was koalas, one year it was white alligators, and one year it was naked mole rats, described in Zoo cheeky promotional blurbs as being "frisky, rare, and seriously ugly."

When he was diagnosed with pancreatic cancer in July 1991, he had already taken steps to begin the transition of authority to those under him in time for his retirement in five years. Instead he died four months later. "He was the match and we were his rockets," said one of his young lieutenants. "He would light us and then watch if we took off or exploded." The Zoo took off during Donaldson's tenure, and during the yearlong search for a replacement, everyone knew that no one could really replace him as a personal force. His successor was named thirteen months later in December 1992. Like Donaldson, he had had no direct experience in zoo administration. Like Donaldson, he came from a nuts and bolts, keep-the-city-moving job in municipal government. Like Donaldson, he got rave reviews after his break-in period as president. Unlike Donaldson, however, something terrible happened one night that changed everything forever.

Donaldson focused on increasing the Zoo's profile in the business and political community, as well as rejuvenating the Zoo's moribund membership rolls. When he arrived at the Zoo in 1979, there were only seven thousand dues-paying Zoo members (an increase of only five thousand since 1874). By 1987, there were thirty-five thousand Zoo member households. Today there are more than fifty thousand.

Donaldson targeted other underutilized fundraising arms of the Zoo such as the Adopt-an-Animal Program, which the year he arrived brought in income of less than $10,000. By 1987, Adopt-an-

Right:
Ben Benson of KYW with Miss Beast and Monty Simmons on KYW Day in June 1952.

Lions by the moat of the treeless grotto soon after the opening of the new Carnivora House.

Left:
Fred Ulmer, curator of
mammals, enters a cave
seeking bats, 1952.

Below:
The annual release of the
flamingos, April 1953.

Above:
RCA Day, July 1953.

Right:
Phil Sheridan,
Pandora the chimp,
and John Regan on
May Day 1953.

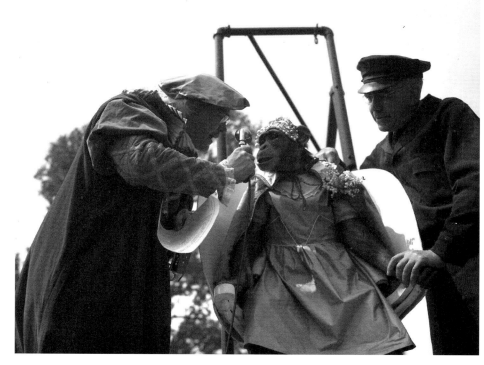

Above:
Kossy the chimp and Willie the Worm, puppet host of a kids' TV show, peek in on a hippo in December 1953.

Left:
A Sumatran tiger cub is curious about Nipper, the RCA dog, on RCA Day in July 1953.

Right:
These Siberian tigers, about two years old in this October 1955 photo, were purchased from Louis Ruke, Inc. They are reputed to be wild-caught in the Amur River Valley.

Below:
Visitors view the monkeys in their indoor cages at the Monkey House in April 1955.

Left:
Chief Halftown and friends.

Below:
Chief Halftown on Monkey Island on May Day 1956.

Above:
Monkey enclosure at
Children's Zoo on May
Day 1957.

Right:
Bactrian camel, 1956.

Left:
***Dedication of Elephant
Statue.***

Below:
***Noah's Ark was one of
the attractions at the
Children's Zoo in 1957.***

Gina Wilson with aardvark.

The Gorilla Statue is installed on the outside of the Rare Mammal House.

RARE MAMMALS

"Talking Story Books," key-operated audio information machines at the Zoo, were inaugurated on a WFIL-TV newscast in 1960.

A horse is a horse, of course, of course—Mr. Ed of TV fame.

Dick Clark, host of "American Bandstand," opens Monkey Island for the season on some Day 1961.

145

Jewel of the Jungle: *Coiled around this tree branch, the water-beaded green tree python seems to shimmer in the light in the Reptile House.*

Curious Serpent: *This green anaconda in the Reptile House seems interested in reading about the endangered status of its species.*

Green anaconda
Eunectes murinus
Northern South America

SPECIES IN DANGER

Reaching lengths of 30 feet and weighing more than 300 pounds, anacondas are one of the largest predators in South America and the heaviest snake in the world. Waterfowl and young crocodiles are potential meals for an anaconda, but they even snatch monkeys from branches hanging over the water.

Copyright © by Tom Hartman.

Who You Calling Bug-Eyed? *This red-eyed tree frog can walk on walls or any other surface. It's among the hundreds of amphibians now on in the Reptile House.*

That you Louie? *Before becoming the stars of certain beer commercials, panther chameleons (bottom left) like this one in the Reptile House were better known for changing color.*

Mohawk Head: *Ever alert for a passing meal, this green water dragon (below) cocks his head to take a closer look.*

Copyright © by Tom Hartman.

Copyright © by Tom Hartman.

Pachyderm People

It's 8:30 on a cool, bright, lose-the-jacket-by-ten-o'clock September morning and the elephant keepers are putting their four-ton charges through their daily ablutions. Brian McCampbell is scraping the dry rough dead skin off the African elephant's back with a rake, while Lynn Fulton is spraying the Indian elephant in the face with a water hose. "This is the most important thing you're seeing right now, this time between the elephants and the keepers," says Tim Hendrickson, the Zoo's elephant-and-camel-ride concessionaire, who can be found in the Elephant House most mornings before the Zoo opens. We're standing on opposite side of the two-inch-thick floor-to-steel-beam poles that separate the elephants from the public. The bars are bowed outward in the middle, evidence of the elephants' power. Inside the bars, the keepers murmur instructions so softly they cannot be heard from fifteen feet away, but the elephants instantly obey. "They've got big ears, right?," explains Hendrickson.

After having sprayed its body with water, Lynn orders the Indian elephant to get lower so she can hose down the top of its head. The Indian elephant lowers itself to its front knees, then leans forward with its trunk to the floor so its rear feet are off the ground. Lynn directs the water spray to the top of elephant's massive skull and back. As the Indian elephant is getting its morning shower, the African elephant rocks back and forth like a puppy that wants to go out, its trunk swinging from side to side in anticipation. Brian works gingerly around the perimeter of the great beast with a shovel and a wheelbarrow, removing its most recent watermelon-sized deposits out from underfoot. It's amazing how clean the elephants' living quarters are considering the frequency and volume of their bowel movements. The whitewashed walls on the opposite side of the elephants' enclosures are pockmarked with round, fist-sized splotches from

hurled elephant poop. "The elephants throw it at people who bother them by tapping on the windows," Hendrickson explains. "They've got pretty good aim with those trunks." The Indian elephant holds up her right foot to allow Lynn to scrub its toenails. Meanwhile Brian is cleaning the African elephant's ivory tusks with a brass wire brush, the kind you buy from Pep Boys to clean whitewall tires. Sometimes the keepers treat the elephants dry scaly skin by scrubbing them down with neat's-foot oil, the same stuff little boys use to break in a new baseball glove (the big difference being that unlike a boy and his glove, after a neat's-foot oil treatment a keeper will not stick his elephant under the mattress overnight).

The keepers use the elephants' given names, but they discourage the public from doing the same. "How would you like a bunch of people calling your name all day long?," asks Hendrickson. "You'd get tired of it, right?" For that reason, the concessionaire tells the people who ask the name of his riding elephant, an African elephant named Bette, that her name is Ella. That way the elephant won't turn or stop at the sound of its name. "We stopped using names in the last few years, and it's cut down on incidents," he says.

Adam Cheek has joined Brian inside the elephants' enclosure and the two keepers begin working with the Indian elephant, which they have been teaching to step on two twelve-inch-square half-inch thick plywood squares in preparation for what the elephants must do to be weighed in a few weeks. Adam stands on the elephant's right next to its ear and gives a command. "Split," he says, and the Indian elephant raises its left front and right rear leg, holding it until Adam says, "Switch." Then the elephant reverses the legs that are lifted. "Good girl," says Adam, producing a treat from his pocket and putting it into the elephant's open mouth.

The African elephant goes through the same plywood square, leg lift training session, repeating the routine three times until, consciously or

Bathtime for the elephants as keepers Lynn Fulton and Mike Seeley look on.

unconsciously, she ends that morning's training session by pooping on the rear plywood square. After cleaning up, the keepers return to the Indian elephant who is being trained to pick up sticks or dowels of increasingly narrow gauge with her trunk. She starts by picking up a stick one-half-inch in diameter, then one a quarter-inch in diameter, and finally a piece of rope. The rope hold doesn't come easily. "Hold it! Hold it!," says Adam, curling the rope around the finger-like gripping end of the proboscis. Once the elephant has hold of the rope, Adam gives it a tug to make sure the hold is secure. "Good girl," he says, slipping another treat in her mouth. Only the Indian elephant is being taught the stick-rope trick in preparation for eventually "tailing up," holding the tail of the elephant walking in front of it. The African elephant won't need that skill since, as the dominant of the two, it will always walk in front.

A little before 9:30, the freshly scrubbed elephants are led outside where they will spend the rest of their day. Within minutes, both elephants will have covered themselves with dust and dirt tossed by their trunks to protect their skin from hot rays of the sun, as if September in Philadelphia was equatorial Africa or the Indian subcontinent.

The African is the dominant elephant despite being outweighed by a thousand pounds (8,850 to 7,850) by the Indian elephant, who at forty-three, is eight years older. Both arrived at the Zoo within a year of their births. The African Elephant spent her infancy at the Children's Zoo, but she's never lost her natural edge. "She's more intense," says Lynn. "She's quicker, but that's the nature of African elephants. They're more—I don't know if you'd say they're nervous, but they're always on the move. Asian elephants, let's face it, they've been domesticated for centuries.

"Since she's the dominant elephant, the African is more acute as far as listening to things that are going on. If the Indian elephant lies down, the African will stand by her, stick with her

Kifaru, a male black rhino, has his horn shaved down by John Regan, Pat Menichini, and Fred Ulmer in 1949.

Leaping Lorikeets!
*The colorful and friendly
Australian lorikeets in the
Lorikeet House will fly onto
the bead, band, shoulder,
or arm of anyone offering
a cup of nectar.*

Here's Looking at You, Kid!
*Talk about eyes devouring a bead—
this slender loris in the Small
Mammal House seems to be nothing
but iris and pupils.*

Sugar Frosted Fox?
This rare red panda from the Himalayas is curled up against the Philadelphia snow in the Carnivore Kingdom.

So Who Needs Snow?
Neither rain, nor sleet, nor hail will keep Coldilocks the polar bear from frolicking in her Bear Country pool.

"She was ninety pounds then. Now she's three thousand pounds." The youngster named Penny, shares an enclosure with her mother Xavera (her father, Billy, died within a week from becoming the oldest breeding rhino in captivity). Two enclosures away, separated by the tapir, Bright Eyes, is Penny's betrothed, a four-year-old male Indian rhino named Sanjay. Their introduction with intention of reproduction awaits an approval by the people in charge of the Indian rhino SSP (Species Survival Plan). "There are only two thousand one-horned Indian rhinos left in the world," Brian says. "And ninety of them are in captivity." The situation among certain species of African rhinos is even more perilous. "I heard a news story years ago that has stuck with me. It said, 'Half the population of white African rhinos died last night. One of them was shot.'"

What's the difference between a rhino and an elephant. "Elephants are herd animals," says Brian. "They'll look kind of like they would in the wild. If an elephant lies down, the other elephants stand watch over them. The Indian elephant will usually lie down by the swimming pool in the hotter months to take a cat nap—or an elephant nap. And the African elephant will stand with her back to the Indian and keep a watch out.

"The Indian elephant is more vocal. She responds to attention. She just loves to be with people. The African is not as affectionate as the Indian elephant. She'll come up to you but it's usually to see if you have food. She's not vocal at all. The African elephant rumbles when she acknowledges your existence. But the Indian will chirp, she 'ughs' and sort of [Adam makes puppy dog whining noise]. Yeah, like a dog almost," Lynn says. Inside the Pachyderm House, Brian is looking at the "baby" rhino born four years ago. "I used to be able to pick this one up," he says.

Pat Menichini, Petal the elephant, unidentified child, and Gordon Scott, new star of Tarzan movies, in 1959.

When the Indian elephant lies down for an afternoon nap, the African stands over her.

four baby warthogs that are the temporary charges of the elephant keepers. The warthogs had to be removed from their mother shortly after their birth to protect them from their father. Brian is outside the pen explaining the dynamics of warthog parenting when the Indian elephant begins chirping from the edge of the stone wall surrounding the outdoor elephant enclosure. "I've gotta be careful not to spend too much time with one elephant or the other gets jealous," says Brian. "The same goes if they see me with other animals." The Indian is more vocal than the African, but both elephants are capable of loud trumpeting or bellowing when excited or alarmed. "It's something that we all come running when we hear it," says Brian.

Inside the outdoor enclosure, the African elephant is digging in the dirt with her trunk in a mudhole near the middle of the yard. "The mudhole used to be close to the wall, but we had to move it because the elephants had a tendency to *share* with people," says Brian. "Not that they did it *on purpose*," he smiles. Elephants do tend to throw missiles, be they made of gravel, stones, dirt or poop, with unerring accuracy. Many mornings the elephant keepers will arrive to find the

for an alpha leader to follow, like a dog. Rhinos are more like cats. Ever try to train a cat?" Like house cats, rhinos will tend to leave you alone. Hippos, on the other hand, would like nothing more than to take a bite out of the hand that feeds it. "We don't go in [inside their enclosure] with them," Brian says of the Zoo's two hippos, sisters Cindy and Una. "They're too unpredictable. Cindy is a good ole girl, but Una, I wouldn't trust her. She only lets you get your hand close to her because it's close to her mouth."

"The best way I can put it is that their ideas of play and my ideas of lay are two different things," says Adam. "They are the only animals in their building we don't go in with," says Lynn. "They are very aggressive by nature." "Hippos can kill you," says Adam. "And they're fast," says Lynn. "They're not slow. They are very basic. In nature all they do is protect their territory, and eat, and have babies and eat, that's it. There's nothing else to them. They're very social. They like to be in groups together, touching each other, but they are constantly squabbling with each other. They're just very aggressive. They bite and chase each other all the time."

Outside the south end of the Pachyderm House in a small grassy area separating it from the Lion House is a fenced-in pen holding the

Unlike most four-legged animals, elephants' legs bend at the knee like humans'.

Bite Me, Just Try It!
This poison dart frog in the Reptile House gets its name from the poisonous secretions in its brilliant blue skin that protect it from predators.

Double Trouble? *This Galapagos tortoise (below) seems twice the animal he is when reflected in the pool in the outdoor enclosure at the Reptile House.*

Copyright © by Tom Hartman.

How's It Hanging? *Egyptian fruit bats (right) share an enclosure with the endangered Rodriguez fruit bats in the Rare Animal House.*

How's the Weather Up There?

It's easy for giraffes to get away from it all, standing eighteen feet tall as they do. This one sleeps inside a cleverly disguised enclosure in African Plains, Phase One.

Quite a Pair!

These frisky giant river otters (below) in the Carnivore Kingdom are a constant favorite with visitors.

Copyright © by Max Lieberman

Cubbyhole: *These red panda cubs (right) can escape the cold in a heated cage hidden away in a rock facing in the Carnivore Kingdom.*

Copyright © by Tom Hartman

Photo by F. Williamson

Photo by Isabelle Hunt.

rhinos and their enclosures splattered with elephant dung tossed at them during the night. "If they're still hungry after they've finished eating their hay for the night, the rhinos have a habit of banging their horns into the doors looking for more," says Lynn. "This must annoy the elephants because in the morning you'll find a straight line of thrown poop leading from the elephants to the rhinos."

Life in the Pachyderm House is never dull.

Hippopotamuses in the old
Elephant House yard. Note
the split rail fences.

Above:
Indian rhinos Penny and Xavera.

Below:
Hippo family members in 1957, left to right, are Marie, month-old-baby Augusta, and Jimmy.

Photo by Isabelle Hunt.

When his new mate arrived in a box in 1950, Jimmy was curious.

Help Me, Pop!
Kiazi the baby colobus monkey seems to be asking his father Springer for a helping hand.

Ole Blue, Blue Eyes: *Not for nothing are Bardot and Redford, at the Lemur Lookout, called blue-eyed lemurs.*

Curious Georges: *The two orange babies (left) at the Rare Animal House are the newest additions to the Zoo's spectacled langur family.*

An A&D Story

It's eleven o'clock on a Thursday morning in late October and most of the senior members of the Animal Department are gathered around the table in the second-floor conference room at the Penrose Building for the bimonthly Acquisitions and Dispositions meeting, A&D for short. It is here that the decisions are made about which animals the Zoo will buy, borrow, sell, exchange, or loan out for breeding purposes. The first animal up for discussion is the Malaysian tapir that has been in the Zoo's collection for eight years and which the Zoo is considering transferring to a commercial wildlife preserve to become the mate of another tapir. But first the Zoo must receive approval for the transfer from the Rotterdam Zoo, which lent the tapir to Philadelphia in the first place.

Or so they thought.

Karl Kranz, senior vice president for animal affairs, chairs the meeting and begins by explaining to his colleagues that there has been a misunderstanding regarding the tapir. After sending a letter to the Rotterdam Zoo seeking approval to transfer the tapir, the Dutch zoo officials responded by saying that according to their records, the tapir wasn't a loan but rather a donation. In other words, it's not our tapir, it's your tapir. Kranz took an Alexandrian approach to what could have been a Gordian knot of paperwork retrieval. "OK," he said, "so I'm asking for approval to receive a donation of a tapir from the Rotterdam Zoo eight years ago."

So moved. Next?

Around the table from Kranz's left sat Beth Bahner, animal collections manager; Kim Whitman, curator of large mammals; Barbara Toddes, nutrition program manager; Lisa Leete,

At an Acquisitions and Dispositions meeting are (below left) John Ffinch, Aliza Baltz, Keith Hinshaw, Andy Baker, and Karl Kranz, and (above) Karl Kranz, Beth Bahner, Barbara Toddes, and Kim Whitman.

director of the Children's Zoo; Aliza Baltz, curator of birds; Ron Fricke, director of group programs and travel; Dr. John Trupkiewicz, director of pathology; Dr. Keith Hinshaw, senior Zoo vet and vice president for animal health; John Ffinch, curator of birds and husbandry; and Dr. Andy Baker, curator of small mammals and primates. Seated on the periphery of the overcrowded table were Reg Hoyt, senior vice president for conversation and science; Dr. Donna Ialeggio-Pelletier, associate veterinarian; and Dr. Kevin Wright, curator of reptiles and amphibians.

There is a lot of laughter amid the serious discussion. Kranz reads a letter of reference regarding the reputation of the manager of a wildlife refuge which is seeking to purchase one of the Zoo's mole rats. The reference letter from someone who had worked with the man in the past is brutally candid and biting. "Wow, pick a tough subject," it began. "[The man in question] has never been, nor will he ever be considered a people person. His philosophy is to win at all costs or at least to always control the situation. He would handle people like elephants. He would ask them nicely once, and if he didn't immediately get the results he wanted, he would immediately badger, threaten and otherwise abuse people into doing what he wanted."

From behind Kranz, Kevin Wright interjects, "Can we hire him?"

After the laughter subsides, Kranz continues reading from the letter, which concludes—to another chorus of laughter—"Good luck on your decision." The discussion roams around the table. Clearly the guy sounds unlikable, but is that the issue? Wright says he's uncomfortable with the description of the personality in the letter. Reg Hoyt says the man's quality of animal husbandry is the question, not his personality. Beth Bahner notes that the letter includes no criticism of his concern for animal welfare. Kranz mentions that he doesn't personally know the man who wrote the reference letter. Kim Whitman questions the wildlife refuge's guarantee of contraception, since there are other animals from the same brood as

Llamas outside Solitude.

the specimen in question. And all this over the sale of a mole rat.

Kranz ends the discussion before a decision is made, saying he would seek more information regarding the wildlife refuge, as well as its commitment not to breed this animal with its broodmates.

Next on the agenda is the proposed disposition of a sloth bear named Nicholas to a conservation center in Kansas. "How are we going to get it there?," asks Kranz. "I don't know," says Bahner. "Perhaps in an aluminum cage used for big cats." Someone offers a wisecrack about packing the sloth bear in Styrofoam peanuts.

Next John Ffinch talks about the transfer of a humboldt penguin to the Akron Zoo. This is followed by Wright describing the acquisition two days earlier of a timber rattlesnake found by Philadelphia police at the scene of a homicide.

The reptile curator assured his colleagues that "the snake's fingerprints were not found on the murder weapon." Timber rattlesnakes are a protected species in Pennsylvania and the Zoo will keep it, as they do all poisonous reptiles brought in by police or SPCA. "Unfortunately, it's a male," says Wright. "We've been looking for a female."

Next comes the disposition of the white alligator that is finishing up its limited and crowd-boosting engagement at Carnivore Kingdom and will be returned to the Audubon Zoo in New Orleans. Then comes the disposition of dozens of the popular lorikeets to their winter quarters. Lisa Leete talks about the acquisition of a African hedgehog, and then mentions the need to thin the number of males in the flock of mallard ducks at the Children's Zoo. It seems the males have been overzealous in the courtship rituals.

Andy Baker talks about the acquisition of a Guyanese squirrel monkey, at a cost of $900 apiece. "Whoa!," says Reg Hoyt at the high cost. "And those animals are treated as pests in Guyana and Surinam."

Kim Whitman talk about the upcoming disposition of one of the Zoo's giraffes. She asks Zoo vet Keith Hinshaw if the giraffe will need an injection of "happy drug" to make the transfer to the shipping crate. Hinshaw says that the giraffe is the best tempered one that the Zoo has ever had, but he's not sure of the dosage of tranquilizer that might be needed.

Finally Kevin Wright reports on the ongoing dispute regarding a shipment of king cobras that is long overdue. He said his threats of legal action against the supplier have resulted in a promise that three king cobras would to be delivered to the Zoo for the price of two. "They're sup-posed to be Thai cobras, but they'll probably be hybrids," Wright says.

"Thai-brids?" jokes Hoyt, to another round of laughter. And so it goes for an hour and a half, serious business leavened by collegial banter. In the end the only unresolved issue was about the sale of the mole rat. "I'm less interested in the character reference than the site reference," Kranz says afterward. "In the end, you can be a jerk and still take good care of animals. But it does give pause."

Two of Primate Reserve's newest acquisitions are young orangutans Mango (right) and Tua (below).

Pete Hoskins, 1993.

THE PRESIDENT'S STORY

PHILADELPHIA
ZOO
AMERICA'S FIRST ZOO

Every Saturday and Sunday during the Zoo's high season from April through September, one member of the senior administrative staff is always in the garden serving as duty officer just in case all hell breaks loose, or a situation develops calling for someone in charge. On this particular Sunday in August the duty officer is Pete Hoskins, president and chief executive officer of the Zoo, who is making the rounds of the Talking Storybooks around the garden to check and see if they are operational. "Kids love these elephant keys," says Hoskins, brandishing a gold plastic key and sticking the elephant trunk into the key slot on the Storybook outside the hippo enclosure. "But they can break off inside the lock or the kids keep turning the key when they don't have to." The Hippo Storybook is working fine, and Hoskins marks it down on the sheet and clipboard he's carrying. One down, thirty-two Talking Storybooks to go.

Hoskins has a friendly, still boyish face after more than a quarter century of working in a variety of posts in Philadelphia municipal government since graduating college with a master's in public administration and moving east from his native California. He first became intimately acquainted with the Zoo as executive director of Fairmount Park from 1980 to 1988, years that coincided with the arrival at the Zoo of the dynamic Bill Donaldson. "I'd come up with my crazy ideas for the park," Hoskins says of Donaldson, "and he'd make them crazier."

CHAPTER EIGHT

Bill Donaldson in Santa suit.

After checking with his boss, Mayor Ed Rendell—"He said, 'The Zoo?! Oh, man, I wish I could do that!' He was excited for me."—the streets commissioner felt free to apply for the zoo job. Methodical, as is his nature, Hoskins tried to find out everything he could about zoos in general and Philadelphia in particular. "Part of my interview process was reorganizing the capital plan," he says.

In January 1993 Alexander L. "Pete" Hoskins took over the reins of the Zoo from the formidable collective memory of Bill Donaldson, who in death still seemed larger than life. It was like Santa Claus retiring and turning over the toy factory at the North Pole to his favorite nephew. You could almost hear the departing sleigh bells greeting Donaldson's successor. But what the new president found was a zoo in debt and in trouble. "In Bill's decade, he couldn't overcome decades of neglect," says Hoskins. "And I mean decades." The physical plant was crumbling, the Zoo was already in two million dollars of debt, and the institution's accreditation with the American Zoo and Aquarium Association was in peril because of a badly needed upgrade of the Zoo's animal hospital.

When Hoskins moved back to city government as streets commissioner, the first nonengineer to hold that post, his almost daily contact with Donaldson continued because of their close work together in finding a solution to the city's trash crisis during the second term of Mayor W. Wilson Goode. The mayor had appointed Donaldson to head the Trash Committee, and Hoskins credits the committee's success with saving the city $200 million over five years of trash disposal. Toward the end of Donaldson's fatal illness, "the only thing he had energy to talk about was the trash deal," Hoskins says.

So how does the streets commissioner become president of the Zoo? Hoskins had to look no farther than his mentor Donaldson to see how someone could move from an apparently unrelated job—city manager of Cincinnati—to the top job at the Philadelphia Zoo. Is a zoo not a city to itself? Are the services required not similar—police, medical, educational, maintenance, capital improvements? Just because some of its citizens weigh tons, while others weigh ounces, doesn't mean they don't need to be fed and housed adequately. "For twenty years I had been working in interdisciplinary jobs," Hoskins says about applying for the zoo job. "I thought, somehow there's something right about this."

This was a critical juncture for the Zoo, and it set a tone for the type of decisions that would be made by the administration and the Board in the years to come. What faced the decision makers was a choice between getting by or making a statement about the future. The present medical facility could be upgraded for $1.5 million, or the Zoo could invest $5.2 million in a new state-of-the-art Animal Health Center. The Zoo chose the latter, and the veterinary staff moved in to the sparkling new facility next to the old Penrose Building in August 1998.

Hoskins went to work on a new plan for a much-needed educational center. The Shelly Building was simply too small to accommodate everything that was being attempted there, from raising endangered baby terrapins in the basement to teaching kindergarteners

Shelly Administration Building, built in 1978.

on the first floor along with housing the docent offices and reception areas to providing office space for marketing, finance, travel, special events, and other executive offices on the second floor. Hoskins succeeded in garnering a $5.4 million appropriation from city and state funds, and in 1995 the William Penn Foundation approved a quarter-million-dollar grant for the creation of a master plan to take the Zoo into the first two decades of the new millennium. The Board of Directors of the Philadelphia Zoological Society met in December 1995 to hear about the new master plan. But before their next meeting, the Zoo would be stopped dead in its tracks by the fire that claimed its prized collection of primates.

In all of the best of times and worst of times that the Philadelphia Zoo has enjoyed or suffered, none was quite so exquisitely painful and enormously inspiring as the fire and its aftermath. The Zoo was tested as never before, and no one was tested more personally than Pete Hoskins. The second guessing, whisper campaigns, and outright accusations of lax management began soon after the fire, and none so forcefully as in the press. Hoskins had enjoyed a relatively favorable relationship with the city's news

media since entering public life, but now he found himself on the receiving end of harsh criticism.

Suddenly a combination of decades-old problems and the coincidence of unfolding events were presented to the public with what could only be described as enormously negative spin. To top it off, Hoskins found himself in the gunsights of a faction of the Board of Directors that were on the verge of open revolt over some of his plans for the future. "This is where I needed faith in myself," Hoskins says of the postfire firestorm in the media and the rebellion on the Board.

Whenever he had doubts, Hoskins focused on the level of emotion that had poured from the public from virtually the entire country in the wake of the tragedy at the World of Primates. Never had he realized how important, how loved, these animals were. Never had it been so clear to him how important the Philadelphia Zoo was in the lives of countless millions. It was humbling and energizing. After a public vote of confidence by Mayor Rendell through his

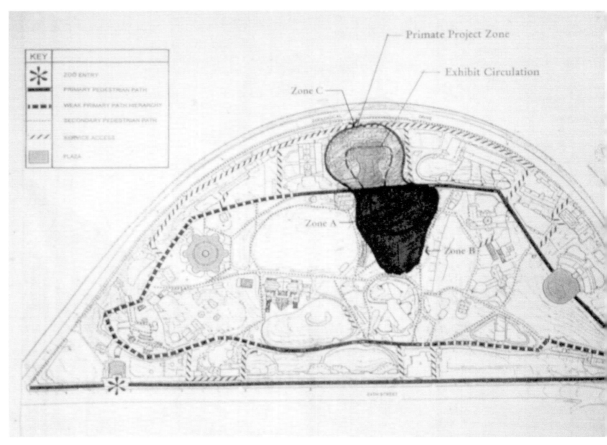

KEY

* ZOO ENTRY

PRIMARY PEDESTRIAN PATH

WEAK PRIMARY PATH HIERARCHY

SECONDARY PEDESTRIAN PATH

SERVICE ACCESS

PLAZA

Primate Project Zone

Exhibit Circulation

Zone C

Zone A

Zone B

The shaded portion of this map shows the area occupied by Primate Reserve.

Primate Reserve under construction.

chief of staff David Cohen, "Neither the mayor nor I subscribed to the view that the problem with the zoo is Pete Hoskins," Cohen told the *Inquirer* in June 1996. "He has struggled valiantly and we have confidence that the Zoo Board with Pete Hoskins can manage its way out of this problem." Hoskins planned for the future with renewed vigor and purpose.

The president returned to the Board with a recommendation that the World of Primates not be rebuilt. "I thought it would be a crime to open the old building after the fire," Hoskins says. "Why not anticipate the next environment rather than go back to the old days." Although the World of Primates had been one of the Zoo's newer exhibits, not even ten years old at the time of the fire, its limitations were apparent to both the public and the keeper staff. Instead of rebuilding the World of Primates at a cost of $5 million, Hoskins urged the Board to think big—$24 million big—for the construction of a Primate Reserve that would not only be state of the art, but it would establish what the state of the art was. "The new Primate Reserve," said Hoskins, "will be the model for everything else we do."

The Board of Directors literally leaped on board the project. Instead of merely replacing the World of Primates for perhaps $6 million, or improving it greatly for twice that amount, the Board voted for the full monty. "If we want to be the best, we've got to act like the best," says Barry Lyngard, Board chairman.

In September of 1996, nine months after the fire, Mayor Rendell addressed the Zoo Board, urging an aggressive construction schedule for the new Primate Reserve, while pledging continued financial support from the city. Then in the spring of 1997, Hoskins convened a three-day "Vision Statement" conference at the Academy of Music consisting of eighty "stakeholders" representing various constituencies served by and serving the Zoo, from employees to academics, from visitors to city officials. "I wanted them to seriously consider basic questions about the Zoo, starting with, 'Should we stay here?'" Hoskins says. Why not move to some two-hundred-acre plot in the far suburbs, rather than try to continually resuscitate a modest forty-two acres in the city with troublesome parking and an aging infrastructure. The answer was clear: stay put. "We're America's first zoo and we'll always be America's first zoo unless we leave," Hoskins says. One of the strengths of the Zoo, the conference attendees agreed, was its central location near

Board Chairman Barry Lyngard.

the heart of Center City. The second thing Hoskins asked the conference to think about was the assumption that the forty-two acres of the Philadelphia Zoo would continue to look the way it does. Currently 38 percent of the Zoo grounds are taken up in exhibit space, the master plan calls for increasing that total to 50 percent. How that is done, Hoskins says, "will challenge or affirm where America's first zoo is going, while maintaining the look of the first zoo in America." The spirited discussion during the Vision conference lead to a number of broadly worded statements of conviction regarding the continuing mission of the modern Zoo, while celebrating its original Victorian character.

On this day as Hoskins checks the Talking Storybooks for sounds of silence, the groan of construction equipment is absent from the rising profile of Primate Reserve inside its fenced-off worksite (it is, after all, a Sunday). Visitors walking past stop to ask directions of the friendly man in a green short-sleeved shirt with the circular Zoo emblem on its breast. Little do they realize that the mild-mannered man giving these directions is also directing Philadelphia's historic Zoo into the most ambitious period of development in more than a century.

Ann Hess communes with a baby gorilla at the Rare Animal House.

QUESTIONS ANYONE?

How much does it cost to feed all the Zoo's animals every day? What do they do with all the poop? Who names the animals? What's the best job at the Zoo? What qualifications does a keeper need? Why don't the big birds fly away? What animal is most dangerous to humans? What is a keeper's biggest nightmare? Do Zoo people feel guilty about keeping the animals in cages? Who would win a fight between a lion and a tiger? Can an elephant cry? What's with all the initials? Who would win a fight between a man and a bobcat? What is the most frequently asked question at the Zoo one day of the year? How many more neck vertebrae does a giraffe have than a mouse? Pound for pound, what is the most expensive animal to feed? What is the name of that stick the elephant keepers use? Why are there no chimpanzees? How much food do the pigeons and other birds steal from the other animals? If a lion and a tiger had a baby, what would it be called? What question from the public do zookeepers hate most? Why is it so easy to get lost in the Zoo? What is the one thing that Zoo people do that Zoo people want you to know?

Believe it or not, I can tell you the answer to all but one of those questions (most of which are in the book, you could look it up). What I can't tell you is what the best job is at the Zoo, because I met too many people who claimed that their job was the best. For them. That's the kind of people we're dealing with here. For the most part, researching this book was like parachuting into Middle Earth and hobnobbing with the elves of Gondor. Remember your *Lord of the Rings?* The elves were the good guys and Gondor was their fortress city, that last outpost of might and light resisting the gathering and irresistible darkness. Zoo people are elves mostly (although I have seen at least one hobbit and perhaps a troll or two. But they could have been vice presidents). And like elves everywhere, they have their own language. Sometimes Zoo people have trouble making themselves understood to humans, because of their elfin dialect, with its abbreviations and unspoken understandings. But I began to appreciate a simple fact that, in general, this is a place where the good guys dwell. They care. They aren't in it for the money. They believe in their mission. Among themselves they talk shop constantly, passionately and intelligently. And they know that they *are* different. Special. Maybe even a little lucky to work where they work.

If you work at the Zoo, it's not like you can tell off the boss, walk out the door, and take a job working for the *next* Syberian tiger down the street. The Philadelphia Eagles have more turnovers in a single season than the Zoo has job vacancies for animal keepers in an entire year. The people who work here like the animals they work for. They work hard. But who's complaining? They've been zoomatized. That's what Umar Mycka calls the process of becoming more than just an employee of the Zoo. Umar, born Joseph Matthew Mycka, who joined the Zoo horticultural staff out of high school in 1973, and whose long hair earned him the nickname Caveman among his co-workers, back in the day when everyone had a nickname, explains what it means to be zoomatized. "People can get very caught up in the Zoo. Extremely caught up in it. I don't know whether they come with that idea, but there's so many stories about people who get so caught up in the idea of the Zoo and they, kind of like, get buried in it." Umar was trying to find the words that only a union official for AFCME could try to find to explain why Zoo people work so hard at their jobs. Ask Anita Primo. She's been zoom-

atized and she's thrilled. Admittedly, Anita is the vice president for financial affairs, the kind of young go-getter from the outer suburbs who would be "ized" in any business she worked for (her last job was as a finance officer with a defense contractor—fuses and detonators and explosives, oh my!). Finance is finance, she says, no matter what the company. Debits, credits, bottom line. Strategies, initiatives, master plans. But the Philadelphia Zoo is special. It's special because of the animals. "Believe it or not that is the number one thing around here, animal welfare," says Primo. It's not driven by the dollars. If animal welfare isn't taken care of and isn't the priority, then we're all in the wrong business." In the end, it's the animals. In the beginning, it's the animals. The whole point, is the animals.

We humans love animals. It's the animal in us I guess. We yearn for our wild brethren because they are so beautiful and so wronged. We feel for animals what we don't feel for fellow humans sometimes; fascination, compassion, awe. Which I would argue makes zoos for animals a better place than cities for people. Why? Because of the kind people—*animal people*—people here at the Zoo. America's first, incidentally. But I mentioned that, didn't I?

INDEX

Clark DeLeon is a native Philadelphian who vividly remembers his first visit to the Zoo at the age of four and who vividly remembers not liking it. It could have been because of his bothersome younger brother, but his "Zoo experience" that first time was bad, but not nearly as bad as his father's experience, evidently, because his father recalled that bad experience prefaced with "Remember the last time I took you to the Zoo?" until Clark was fifteen or sixteen. After a childhood spent casing the mean streets of Narberth ("I grew up on a street as tough as its name," he likes to say. "Shirley Circle."), DeLeon graduated Lower Merion High School in 1967, worked in a gas station for two years, then enrolled in Montgomery County Community College. While at community college DeLeon developed an interest in journalism while editor of the student newspaper. At Temple University DeLeon majored in journalism and became a columnist for the daily student newspaper, the *Temple News.* One of the columns he wrote for the paper about assisting in the birth of his son won the national William Randolph Hearst Feature Writing Award. In 1972, DeLeon was hired by the *Philadelphia Inquirer* as a suburban reporter. This began a twenty-three-year career at *The Inquirer.* For twenty of those years, between 1974 and 1994, DeLeon wrote a daily column called "The Scene," which was pretty darn good if he does say so himself. DeLeon was named the city's best newspaper columnist by editors and readers of *Philadelphia* magazine eight times. DeLeon is also a veteran of Philadelphia broadcast media, television and radio. Beginning with the newspaper strike in 1985, DeLeon joined KYW-TV as a feature columnist. In 1988 he was a twice-daily commentator on WOGL-FM, and in 1990 DeLeon hosted a talk show on WCAU-AM Monday through Friday from 1:00 p.m. until 3:00 p.m., at which time Frank Rizzo took over the microphone to do his show from the same studio. DeLeon liked to jokingly refer to his and Rizzo's shows as "Good cop, bad cop" and Rizzo never seemed to mind.

In 1996 DeLeon was hired as the print media critic and general assignment reporter at WCAU-TV, NBC-10. Later he wrote and produced a weekly feature called "Clark's Column" on Channel 10's "Sunday Morning Edition." In 1997, DeLeon began writing a thrice-weekly column on America On Line's "Digital City Philadelphia." (Keyword: Clark) and hosted a weekly hour-long chat on "Digital City Philadelphia" on Tuesday night from 9:00 p.m. until 10:00 p.m.

America's First Zoostory is DeLeon's first book, which he says is about time, as well as its being appropriate since his name is Spanish for "lion," or a reasonable facsimile thereof. Since 1985 DeLeon has lived in West Philadelphia with his wife, Sara, and their three children. He says that since that first visit forty-five years ago, he has gotten to like the Philadelphia Zoo a whole lot. And since he began working on this book, he's gotten to like it a whole lot more.